Peppy Puppet Presentations

65 Short Scripts for Puppeteers

Mark and Donna Skorheim

Baker Books
A Division of Baker Book House Co
Grand Rapids, Michigan 49516

Published by Baker Books,
a division of Baker Book House Company
PO Box 6287, Grand Rapids, MI 49516-6287

Library of Congress Cataloging-in-Publication Data

Skorheim, Mark.
    Peppy puppet presentations : 65 short scripts for puppeteers / Mark and Donna Skorheim.
        p.   cm.
    Summary: Includes scripts for short puppet plays, with such titles as "Dusting for Jesus," "Caught Stealing," "After Church," "Forgive and Forget," and "Why Pray When You Can Worry."
    ISBN 0-8010-8359-1
    1. Puppet plays, American—Juvenile literature. 2. Puppet plays in Christian education—Juvenile literature. [1. Puppet plays. 2. Christian life—Drama.] · I. Skorheim, Donna. II. Title.
PN1980.S46   1993
812'.54—dc20
                                                  93-19351

Printed in the United States of America

Dedicated to Kirk and Susan Hayes
who have been our Barnabas in this endeavor
Acts 4:36

Contents

Cast of Characters

Meet the Green Family

We use in these sketches a family of puppets. The family is called the Green family. All of the puppets are literally green in color. We have received letters from missionaries using the sketches overseas who express delight in the use of the neutral color green in reaching every nationality and race.

If you or your church have difficulty getting an entire family set of puppets or would like a complete green set, we recommend

One Way Street Puppets
P.O. Box 2398
Littleton, CO 80161
(303) 790-1188
Order line 1-800-569-4537.

Please allow 4-6 weeks delivery. Choice of hair color available; clothing may vary.

Let us introduce you to the Green family.

Boy puppet: Charlie Green
Girl puppet: Susie Green

Charlie and Susie are two grade-school kids. They take turns getting into difficult situations or into trouble. They are both fun characters to play because they are rambunctious kids with lots of spunk and humor.

Dad puppet: Mr. Green
Mom puppet: Mrs. Green
Grandpa puppet: Grandpa Green
Grandma puppet: Grandma Green

These are the adults in the Green family. Dad and Mom are usually helping correct and direct Charlie and Susie according to what God's Word teaches about Charlie's or Susie's present circumstance or situation.

Grandpa and Grandma serve as extra adults and characters to offer wisdom and advice. Sometimes, as in real family life, the entire family ends up learning together a lesson from God's Word.

Other Characters:

Dog puppet: Caleb. We named our dog Caleb because it is Hebrew for "dog." If your group of students has a child named Caleb, please be sure to change the dog's name if you think the boy would be offended.

Cat puppet: Methuselah. We named the cat Methuselah because a cat is supposed to have nine lives, and Methuselah is the biblical character with the longest recorded life.

Boy and girl puppets: John and Pam White serve as Charlie and Susie's friends when an additional puppet is needed to teach the lesson for a particular script. They are used very rarely in the sketches. This helps save the cost of two extra puppets if you are on a very limited budget.

A fun idea, if you choose to make your green family of puppets literally green, is to use the song "It Ain't Easy Being Green" by Kermit the Frog as a different introduction in a lighter situation or when Charlie is having an extra difficult time in a sketch.

Other ideas to intersperse for fun are takeoffs on the word *green*.

1. They live in the "Green" house; people think they are a bunch of plants!
2. "Green" thumb
3. Feeling "green" for sick
4. "Green" with jealousy or envy

Hopefully this will get your creative juices flowing. People amaze us with their creative ideas for the Green family.

A difficulty with publication is it is a one-way communication. We would enjoy hearing your creative ideas or how you use the Green family sketches. Our address:

Mark and Donna Skorheim
108 Newport Lane
Bullard, TX 75757

May God bless and multiply your ministry and efforts with puppets.

Some Helpful Hints for Beginners with Puppets

1. Copy the script and mark your lines with a colored highlighter. This makes it easier to follow your lines and to find your place, should you lose it during a presentation.

2. Be careful not to talk up to the ceiling. Your wrist and hand should point in the direction you are talking. Also, do not bob your puppet up and down when it speaks. Give it human actions.

3. Get someone to watch you practice and give suggestions. It also helps to do your presentation in front of a mirror and try ways of helping your puppet take on the emotions of the play.

4. The hardest part of being a good puppeteer is to move the puppet's mouth with its words. This takes practice. Again, watching in the mirror is helpful.

5. Be creative. This might sound trite, but it is easy to follow a script word-for-word out of a book. It takes work to adapt and make it more acceptable to your audience. References to occasions, etc., make the presentation much more personal. We just write them in pencil on the script.

6. Music adds much to a sketch. We often have a person sit behind us and help us with any special effects such as music, props, sound. When they are not busy they help support our arms.

7. If you are on a limited budget we encourage you to use it toward puppets and props and save money for a stage. We still often use a table turned on its side or a long pole with a blanket attached. We get two young people to hold the pole. This works great if you have to travel to a camp and space is limited.

8. One prop we have found useful is a handmover. A handmover is a stiff wire connected to a wooden handle. This wire is about sixteen inches long and can be attached to the puppet's hand. The puppeteer can hold the wooden handle and move the puppet's hand. Puppet handmovers are available at most Christian bookstores that sell puppets.

9. When we do a sketch that takes place in a car, we use a tape of car noises in the background, such as doors slamming or car starting. It is easy to make. Just take a tape recorder and get in your car and drive. If you use this to

establish the car scene, wait for the beginning car noises to stop and puppets to be on the road to begin the sketch dialogue. A good friend prepared a tape for us and happened to get the sound of beginning to drive in a gravel driveway. As the gravel flew and the car took off, all four puppets leaned back. It was a big hit with the kids (and the adults) in the audience.

10. Be careful not to have puppets actually pray or receive Christ in the sketch. Young children could confuse a real spiritual need with something that is imaginary. Later this could cause confusion as to what is real and what is not real.

11. Relax and have some fun. We have found the audience enjoys and often learns the most from how we relate to mistakes. Laugh it off and start over if necessary, using lines such as the following:

This is so much fun, let's do it again.

Stop the camera; take two; are the cameras rolling?

To the other puppet: "Did you hear me?" Puppet: "No." "I didn't think so. Let me repeat it." Then say the last line. This gives the other puppeteer time to find the place in the script.

Have one of the puppets look at the audience and say, "You didn't laugh enough last time. If you don't laugh louder this time you might have to see this presentation a third time." (There is something funny about seeing the beginning of the sketch a second time and knowing the punch line.)

If all else fails, blame it on the puppets. They have broad shoulders and won't talk back!

Dusting for Jesus

Characters

Boy puppet
Girl puppet
Dad puppet

Optional

Dog puppet

Props

A rag with lots of dust or baking soda on it (keep in plastic bag until right before presentation); a puppet hand mover, or a good straight stick attached to SUSIE'S hand

---

SUSIE   *(Comes up with a dust rag attached to her hand, flinging it every which way, giving the idea of haphazard dusting.)*

CHARLIE   *(Comes up gasping for air)* Achoo! Susie, what are you doing? *(Cough)*

SUSIE   I'm dusting.

CHARLIE   It doesn't look like you are doing anything but stirring up the dust.

SUSIE   So what? I just want to be able to tell Mom I dusted so I won't get into trouble when she gets home.

CHARLIE   I know what you mean. I have to go clean my room so I can get my allowance from Dad.

SUSIE   You mean you have to pick up everything in your room and shove it into your closet.

CHARLIE   Right! You got the idea.

SUSIE   I personally like to push all my stuff under the bed. It's much easier.

CHARLIE   Hey, that's a good idea. I think I'll try that this time. My closet is so full I can hardly get the door closed.

SUSIE   I know. I opened the door of your closet yesterday to get a ping-pong paddle, and a baseball fell out and hit Caleb on the head. *(CALEB rubs head and nods yes.)*

CHARLIE   No wonder Caleb won't come in my room anymore. But with your great idea of putting stuff under the bed he won't have to worry. *(CALEB goes over and rubs against CHARLIE.)*

SUSIE   Glad I could help you.

DAD   Charlie and Susie, where are you?

CHARLIE and SUSIE   We're in here.

DAD   I just got off the phone with Mrs. White. She said she hired you two to rake her leaves.

CHARLIE   We did that yesterday. She's already paid us.

DAD   Yes, she said you raked all the leaves out of her yard and onto the street. The wind last night blew them all back into her yard.

SUSIE   Uh oh.

DAD   You both know you should have raked those leaves into bags.

CHARLIE   Well, the wind was blowing the other way yesterday, and we thought it would carry them into someone else's yard.

DAD   Charlie and Susie, you both are not doing your work very well. Did you know the Bible has a verse that is good to remember as you do your work?

SUSIE   What verse is that, Dad?

DAD   It's found in Colossians 3:23. It says, "And whatever you do, do it heartily, as to the Lord, and not to men" (NKJV).

SUSIE   Does that mean our work?

DAD   Yes, everything we do we should do it as if we were doing it for Jesus.

CHARLIE   You mean even raking leaves?

DAD   Even raking leaves, and cleaning our rooms, and dusting. Everything we do. Christians do their best in respect for the people they work for.

That, in turn, is an imitation of Jesus' love and respect for them.

CHARLIE   We had better go over and rake Mrs. White's yard again.

SUSIE   This time we'll put the leaves in bags.

CHARLIE   I want to do a good job, since I'm doing it for Jesus.

SUSIE   Dad, will you call Mrs. White and tell her we will be over in an hour? I need to get some furniture polish from under the sink and do my dusting.

DAD   Yes, I'll call her.

CHARLIE   While you do that, I'm going to go clean my room and my closet.

SUSIE   Uh oh! Dad, you might need to tell Mrs. White we won't be there for quite a while!

DAD   (Chuckle) You're right, Susie. It could take Charlie all day to clean his closet!

CALEB   (Nods head)

(CHARLIE and SUSIE leave).

DAD   I think I'll go read the paper. On second thought, maybe I'd better go clean the garage.

Choosing Friends

Characters

Girl puppet
Boy puppet
Mom puppet
Dad puppet

MOM *(Angrily)* Charrrliee . . . Charrrliee . . . *(CHARLIE appears.)*

CHARLIE Yes, Mom?

MOM Charlie! I just got off the phone with Mr. Brown, your principal. He said you and some other boys were seen throwing rocks at the school after class, and two windows were found broken!

CHARLIE Uh, well, uh, umm. *(DAD enters.)*

DAD Charlie! Our next door neighbor, Mrs. White, said she saw you and some other boys writing with spray cans on a fence in the alley, and some of the words were not very nice!

CHARLIE Uh, well, uh, umm. *(SUSIE appears.)*

SUSIE Charlie! I just saw Jennifer, and she said you and some other boys knocked her off her bike and threw her books all over the street!

CHARLIE Uh, well, uh, umm.

DAD, MOM, and SUSIE: *(In unison)* Charlie! What do you have to say for yourself?!

CHARLIE *(Looks out at boys and girls in audience)* Help!

MOM Charlie Donald, did you do these things?

CHARLIE Uh, well, it really wasn't my fault. Those other guys made me do it.

DAD What other guys?

CHARLIE Some of the guys at school: Spike, Slugger, and Rocky.

SUSIE *(Surprised)* Charlie, what are you doing hanging around with those guys?

CHARLIE Well, after school they asked me if I wanted to go with them and have some fun. I thought they meant play baseball or something like that.

DAD Charlie, answer the question. Did you do all those things?

CHARLIE Yes, I did, but I really didn't want to!

MOM Charlie, it sounds like you feel you had to do these things you didn't want to because of what those boys might say or think.

CHARLIE That's right. I thought those guys might think I'm a sissy or something. I knew those things were wrong.

DAD   Charlie, I think you can learn a good lesson from this experience. Being good is easier when you choose friends who are good.

CHARLIE   I wouldn't have been doing those bad things if I weren't with Spike, Slugger, and Rocky.

DAD   That's right, Charlie.

MOM   A Bible verse, Psalm 1:1, says, "Oh, the joys of those who do not follow evil men's advice, who do not hang around with sinners" (TLB).

CHARLIE   I know, Mom. I didn't have any joy when I was doing what Spike, Slugger, and Rocky said to do.

MOM   Charlie, you're going to have a busy week earning money to pay for the damage done by you and your friends.

DAD   You're also going to be busy telling people you're sorry.

CHARLIE   At least it will help me not to forget to follow what the Bible says to be careful about choosing friends.

SUSIE   Come on, Charlie. I'll walk over to Jennifer's with you so you can apologize.

CHARLIE   Thanks, Susie. You're a *good* sister. I should hang around with you more often.

DAD and MOM   Good boy, Charlie!

Sticks and Stones Versus Ugly Names

Characters

Boy puppet
Girl puppet

Props

Small piece black felt; Band-Aid

CHARLIE   (Comes up with Band-Aid, black eye [one-half circle felt], and hair messed up) (Groans) Oh-h-h . . .

SUSIE   Charlie, what happened to you?

CHARLIE   I was in a fight.

SUSIE   What did you fight with, a lion or a bear?

CHARLIE   Worse. Brutus!

SUSIE   Brutus! My, you are brave! Why did you fight with him?

CHARLIE   He called me a mouse face.

SUSIE   So what else is new? He calls you that all the time.

CHARLIE   I just got tired of hearing, "Mouse face, mouse face, eat your cheese, please."

SUSIE   But Charlie, I've heard you say to him many times, "Sticks and stones may break my bones, but names will never hurt me."

CHARLIE   I know. But Susie, that just isn't true. Every time Brutus calls my desk a rat trap it hurts me.

SUSIE   Even more than the hurt and pain from your black eye?

CHARLIE   Yes. It's inside hurt, but it still hurts.

SUSIE   Charlie, did you know Jesus understands when people hurt?

CHARLIE   How?

SUSIE   Before he died on the cross for the world, the Bible says, some soldiers put a crown of thorns on his head and mocked him.

CHARLIE   How awful! They made fun of Jesus? What did he do?

SUSIE   He didn't say anything. Later he even prayed for them.

CHARLIE   Those people needed prayer if they acted that mean.

SUSIE   Charlie, so does Brutus.

CHARLIE   Brutus needs prayer all right. Prayer that he will shrink!

SUSIE   Jesus says, "Love your enemies, and pray for those who hurt you."

CHARLIE   Pray for your enemies. You mean people like Brutus?

SUSIE   Yes, especially people like Brutus. Sometimes it's not easy to do what Jesus wants. It takes work. It's easy for people to get caught up in the rat race and not pray about problems and difficult people.

CHARLIE   Did you say "rat" race? I hate that word *rat*. It reminds me too much of mouse face.

SUSIE   Oops, sorry!

CHARLIE   Next thing you know, we'll be having macaroni and *cheese* for dinner!

Beauty Is in the Eyes of the Maker

Characters

Girl puppet
Boy puppet
Mom puppet

SUSIE   *(Looking straight ahead into imaginary mirror)* Boy, God did a good job when he created me. *(Toss head)* I love watching my hair fall perfectly in place each time I do this. *(Toss head)*

CHARLIE   *(Knocking sound)* Susie, hurry up. We'll be late for school. I need my turn in the bathroom.

SUSIE   Oh, Charlie, go away. You are hopeless, anyway. You've been hit with an ugly stick, and whoever hit you hit you real hard. Ha! Ha! Ha!

CHARLIE   *(Knocking)* Come on, Susie. I'm going to have to go tell Mom.

SUSIE   Oh, all right. *(Walks by CHARLIE; tosses head)* Charlie, you are going to have to learn that I am the one everyone notices in this family. I don't know why you even bother trying to get ready.

CHARLIE   *(Under breath)* I want to look nice for those moments, Susie, when you're not around. (Down)

MOM   Charlie, Susie, come on. Breakfast is almost ready. You're going to be late for school.

SUSIE   Charlie's coming in a minute. He's in the bathroom. He's such a bathroom hog.

MOM   Now, Susie, let's be kind.

CHARLIE   Susie be kind? That's a new idea.

(SUSIE tosses head)

MOM   All right children. Didn't you learn anything in Sunday school and church yesterday?

SUSIE   Yes. My Sunday school teacher did a wonderful lesson yesterday. She told us how special God made each of us.

MOM   Susie, it's so nice to hear you saying good things about a Sunday school lesson.

SUSIE   Our memory verse was Psalm 139:14: "I will give thanks to Thee, for I am fearfully and wonderfully made; wonderful are Thy works, and my soul knows it very well" (NASB).

MOM   Susie, I'm proud of you for learning your verse.

SUSIE   I always knew I was wonderfully made, but I don't understand why my teacher didn't ask ugly Homer to leave before she taught the lesson.

MOM   God made each person special. God has no favorites. He has a reason and purpose for making each of us just the way we are.

SUSIE   Even Homer?!

MOM   Yes, Susie. To God all of us are beautiful, because he made us. When you make fun of other people and the way they look, you are making fun of something God made.

SUSIE   Oh! I don't want to do that.

CHARLIE   Yesterday, at Sunday school, Gilbert was making fun of the craft I made. I told him he just didn't have any taste, but his teasing made me feel sad.

MOM   That's how God feels when we make fun of others. He feels sad because he knows it hurts the person being teased and someone is making fun of something he has made.

SUSIE   Boy, we sure need to be careful about teasing others. Especially since God made everyone special, even brothers like Charlie.

CHARLIE   Gee, thanks, Susie. I think I'm going to say some nice things today about the people God made.

SUSIE   Mom, I've learned so much already this morning. I don't think I need to go to school.

MOM   Susie, God made our minds to be so wonderful, we can learn more than we could ever imagine.

SUSIE   Oh, well, see you this afternoon.

CHARLIE   Bye, Mom. You look real nice.

MOM   Bye. Remember, God and I both think you are special.

To Obey or Not to Obey . . .

That is the question

Characters

Boy puppet
Girl puppet
Mom puppet
Dad puppet

Props

Nightcap for boy puppet; piece of paper to tear

(*CHARLIE and SUSIE up first, both staring ahead, mouths open*)

DAD   Charlie and Susie! What are you watching? Your mom and I told you that you could not watch that T.V. show.

CHARLIE   Aw, come on, Dad. Everybody else watches this show.

DAD   Charlie, I'm not everybody else's dad. I am *your* dad. Now obey me and change the channel.

(*SUSIE leans forward; clicking noise. DAD leaves. Wait a couple of seconds.*)

MOM   Charlie, Susie, time for bed. Turn the T.V. off now and get ready for bed.

SUSIE   (*Leaving*) Good night, Mom.

CHARLIE   Aw, come on, Mom. Let me watch just one more show.

MOM   No, Charlie, now head to bed.

CHARLIE   Mom, I'm older than Susie. I should be able to stay up later.

MOM   Not on a school night, Charlie. Now obey me and get to bed.

CHARLIE   (*Under breath*) All right. I hate that word *obey*.

(*EVERYBODY down.*)

DAD   Charlie, I came to say good night. (*Dad looks down. CHARLIE doesn't come up. Make sound of ripping paper and throw paper in the air.*) Charlie, what are you doing?

CHARLIE   I'm ripping Ephesians 6:1 out of my Bible.

DAD   Why?

(*CHARLIE comes up with a nightcap on his head.*)

CHARLIE   I hate that verse. "Children obey your parents in the Lord: for this is right" (NKJV).

DAD   Charlie, it's hard to obey, but ripping it out of your Bible won't help. It is still in mine.

19

CHARLIE   How do you know it's hard to obey?

DAD   I have to obey my boss at work. It's not always easy. Sometimes I want to do things my way and I can't.

CHARLIE   Wow! I know how you feel.

DAD   Charlie, God has given to all of us people we are to obey. God tells us to obey the people in authority over us; so when we obey them we are really obeying God.

CHARLIE   You mean when I obey you and Mom, I'm obeying God?

DAD   Yes, Charlie. God wants us to obey. That way we will better learn to obey him and his Word.

CHARLIE   Wow! I never thought of it that way before. Quick! Where is the tape?

DAD   Come on, son. I'll help you tape this verse back in your Bible, and then it's off to bed.

CHARLIE   Yes, sir. I'm learning already, right, Dad?

DAD   Right, son.

And They Call This Vacation?

Characters

Boy puppet
Girl puppet
Mom puppet
Dad puppet

Optional Prop

Tape with car noises

Have the family arranged as if they are sitting in a car, if possible: parents in front, two children puppets behind.

DAD   We're finally off on vacation!

MOM   I hope we haven't forgotten anything. Susie, did you remember your medicine?

SUSIE   Yes, Mom, for the tenth time!

DAD   Susie, don't be smart with your mom. *(Turns toward MOM)* Now don't worry, dear. You always worry too much.

MOM   *(Turns away from DAD):* Hmph! Okay then, I just won't say anything.

(CHARLIE nudges up against SUSIE.)

SUSIE   Charlie! Quit hitting me! Dad, Charlie keeps hitting me!

DAD   Charlie, keep your hands to yourself.

SUSIE   *(Looks over at CHARLIE and whispers)* Ha! Ha! Ha!

DAD   Hey, now everyone, let's have fun. This is our vacation!

CHARLIE   Dad, how much farther? I'm hungry!

MOM   Here, Charlie, have some crackers so I won't *worry* about you starving to death.

DAD   Okay, dear. I'm sorry I said you worry.

MOM   Don't *worry* about it.

SUSIE   Charlie, quit touching me with your foot. Mom, Charlie's touching me.

MOM   Okay, you two, if you don't stop this I'm really going to touch you both on the seat of your pants!

CHARLIE   *(Looks down toward the center)* See that line?

SUSIE   Yes.

CHARLIE   You stay on your side of the seat. Don't you dare cross that line.

SUSIE   What if I do?

CHARLIE   Just try it. You'll see. *(SUSIE crosses over line.)* Dad! Susie won't stay on her side of the car. *(CHARLIE bumps into her.)*

DAD   Okay, you two. If I have to stop this car I'm going to make it worth my while. *(Quiet for three seconds. EVERYONE looks forward.)* Let's turn on the radio. I wonder if we can still get that new Christian radio station.

ANNOUNCER   *(DAD puppeteer in lower voice, or have an announcer read. If puppeteer does it, don't forget not to move the puppet's mouth.)* Now from the Word. Ephesians 4:32: "And be ye kind one to another, tenderhearted, forgiving one another, just as God for Christ's sake hath forgiven you" (KJV). *(Puppets begin hanging heads.)* What a good verse for all of us now that summer is here and it's time for family vacation. I think I will have my family read this verse before we leave.

DAD   I'd better stop the car. Let's pull over here for a minute. *(EVERYBODY lean to the right.)*

CHARLIE   I didn't mean it, Dad.

DAD   Charlie, I'm not going to spank you. We have all been wrong since we left home.

CHARLIE   Let's have Mom write out Ephesians 4:32 and put it on the dash to remind us of how God would want people to act.

SUSIE   That's a good idea, Charlie.

MOM   My Bible! I knew I forgot something! *(ALL exit together.)*

No Will, No Way

Characters

Boy puppet
Girl puppet
Mom puppet

MOM   Hello, Susie. How was school today?

SUSIE   *Awful!* We had to climb ropes for the teacher during play time today. *I can't* do it!

MOM   Susie, you've never climbed ropes before today. You just need to practice. Maybe Dad could help you learn by putting a rope up on the big tree in the backyard.

SUSIE   No need. *I can't* climb ropes. No practice will help.

(MOM goes down. CHARLIE comes up.)

CHARLIE   Hey, Susie-Q. What are you doing?

SUSIE   I was going to do my homework, but *I can't.*

CHARLIE   Why not?

SUSIE   We're doing subtraction in math, and *I can't* do it.

CHARLIE   Do you want me to help you?

SUSIE   No, there's no use. *I can't* learn subtraction.

MOM   Susie. Oh, Susie.

SUSIE   Yes, Mom. What do you want?

MOM   Susie, I just received a phone call from your new Sunday school teacher. She says you are not memorizing your verses.

SUSIE   Mom, *I can't* memorize. I always forget.

MOM   Do you practice the verse during the week?

SUSIE   No, but *I can't* memorize.

MOM   Susie, since you've been home I have heard you say "I can't" in about every sentence.

SUSIE   It's hard being a kid today.

MOM   I know, Susie, but I think this first verse you're supposed to memorize this week will help you. Philippians 4:13: "I can do all things through Christ who strengthens me" (NKJV).

SUSIE   What does that mean?

MOM   Jesus promises to replace "I can'ts" with "I cans" with his help.

SUSIE   Wow, that's a neat verse. Let me see if *I can* say it. *(Haltingly)* "I can do all things through Christ who strengthens me." Now where is it found?

MOM   Philippians 4:13. You did very good, Susie.

SUSIE   I'm going to work on it. Jesus will help.

MOM   Good girl, Susie. My mom used to tell me, "If there's a will, there's a way."

SUSIE   You mean you have to want to do something hard before you can do it?

MOM   Yes, Susie. When you have something difficult to do remember Philippians 4:13 and ask Jesus for help; then get in there and practice and work hard.

SUSIE   I think *I can* do that.

MOM   Good girl. Now come help me set the table for dinner. Dad will be home soon, and you can help him put up a rope in the backyard.

Caught Stealing

Characters

Mom puppet
Boy puppet
Girl puppet

CHARLIE   *(CHARLIE and SUSIE come up together.)* Susie, let's go over to the candy counter while Mom shops.

SUSIE   Sure, we can always look.

CHARLIE   I'm going to buy that candy bar for Tommy. I bet when I give it to him he will really like me.

SUSIE   Charlie, where are you going to get the money to buy candy?

CHARLIE   I've got money, plenty of money. Now, let's see. I'll buy that candy toy for Steve. He'll really think I'm a neat guy.

SUSIE   Wow, Charlie. You must have a lot of money to be getting all this candy. Will you buy me that doll-shaped sucker?

CHARLIE   Sure, but nothing else. I need to save some of my money to let the guys see at school so they'll think I'm cool. I'm really going to be popular now.

(BOTH puppets go down. After a couple of seconds ALL THREE come up.)

MOM   Thanks, kids, for helping me put up the groceries.

CHARLIE and SUSIE   You're welcome.

MOM   Charlie, what's in your sack?

SUSIE   Candy, lots of candy. He bought some for everybody. Even a sucker for me. Boy, is he going to be popular at school!

MOM   Charlie, where did you get the money to buy all that candy?

CHARLIE   I found it.

MOM   Where did you find it, Charlie Donald?

CHARLIE   Well, I sorta found it in Dad's wallet this morning.

MOM   Charlie, that is not finding it. That's stealing.

SUSIE   Is Charlie in trouble?

MOM   Yes, Susie, Charlie has done something wrong. The Bible tells us in Ephesians 4:28 not to steal. Stealing is sin. Now, Susie, you go to your room and play while Charlie and I talk. *(SUSIE leaves.)*

CHARLIE   I'm sorry, Mom. I just wanted everyone to like me, so I bought them candy.

MOM   Charlie, it doesn't matter why you stole the money from Dad's wallet.

Stealing is wrong. When a person steals he needs to tell God he is sorry first. Second, he needs to pay back what he stole.

CHARLIE   Boy, it will be hard to pay back Dad.

MOM   You will have to work out some jobs with your dad. He's going to be disappointed in you.

CHARLIE   You and Dad, and probably Susie, are disappointed in me. I took the money so people would like me. I didn't do very good, did I?

MOM   Son, if you have to steal to impress those people so that they will be your friends, they would not make very good friends, anyway. Now, why don't you take Susie her sucker and tell her you are sorry for being a bad example for her.

CHARLIE   Yes, Mom. I think I'll never forget Ephesians 4:18: "Let him who stole steal no longer" (NKJV).

Sportsmanship

Characters

Dad puppet
Two boy puppets
Girl puppet

Props

Two ping-pong balls

CHARLIE   Hey, Susie, you want to play ball?

SUSIE   Yes, I would like to play ball.

CHARLIE   Good. Here, catch. *(Throws ping-pong ball. You can put ball in puppet's mouth and throw.)*

SUSIE   Oh! I'm sorry, I missed.

CHARLIE   Susie, you sure can't play ball very well. That was really a dumb catch. I should have known. You're *just* a girl. If I ever choose teams to play ball, I'm never choosing you.

SUSIE   I said I was sorry. I'd better go home.

(JOHN enters.)

CHARLIE   Hey! John, want to play ball?

JOHN   Sure, Charlie.

CHARLIE   I'll get the ball. You should see what a terrible player Susie is. She's just plain lousy. Here, catch! *(Throw ball.)*

JOHN   Oops! I missed. Here, let me run and get the ball.

CHARLIE   Never mind. You're worse than Susie. Why don't you go play with the babies in baby school? Ha! Ha! Ha!

(EVERYONE goes offstage.)

CHARLIE   What a nice new day! There's Susie. I think I'll ask her to play ball. Susie, oh Susie, will you play ball with me?

SUSIE   No, thank you, Charlie.

CHARLIE   Well, I didn't want to play with you, anyway. You can't play ball as good as me. I'll see if John wants to play. Hey, John . . . *(knock, knock)*

JOHN   Hi, Charlie.

CHARLIE   Will you play ball with me?

JOHN   No, thank you, Charlie.

CHARLIE   I guess I'll have to go home by myself. No one wants to play with me. I don't understand.

DAD   *(Comes out)* Hi, Charlie. I've been wanting to talk to you. Do you have some time?

CHARLIE   Yes, Dad. No one seems to want to play with me.

DAD   That's what I want to talk to you about. The other day when you were

27

playing ball, you said some pretty ugly things to the referee.

CHARLIE   Well, Dad, he made a bad call. I was safe!

DAD   That's not what we are talking about. The referee did the best he could. Remember, he sees more than you can.

CHARLIE   You're on his side.

DAD   No, Charlie, I'm concerned about your temper. The Bible tells us in Proverbs 19:11: "A man's discretion makes him slow to anger" (NASB).

CHARLIE   I was not slow to anger. I guess I need to apologize to that referee and to Susie and John.

DAD   Yes, Charlie, I think that would be a good idea. I think you will have more friends to play with. No one likes to be around people with a bad temper or a poor sport.

CHARLIE   Thanks, Dad. I'd better go. I have a lot to do, huh?

DAD   Yes, son. I'll see you later.

Listening

Characters

Boy puppet
Girl puppet
Mom puppet

Optional Prop

Fireman's hat for Charlie

SPECIAL INSTRUCTIONS: This sketch takes some practice on the sentences that are interrupted. The puppet being interrupted needs to fade out with the phrase in parentheses and not just stop. There should be no time between these sentences.

CHARLIE   (Say rotelike) "But let every one be quick to hear, slow to speak and slow to anger. James 1:19" (NASB).

SUSIE   Hi, Charlie. What are you doing . . . (this morning)

(Interrupt)

CHARLIE   I'm learning my verse for Sunday school. We get a super-duper prize for memorizing it. It's really not a hard verse to learn.

SUSIE   Did I tell you about the neat verse we . . . (were learning)

(Interrupt)

CHARLIE   I don't have time to listen now. I've gotta learn this verse. James 1:19: "But let everyone be quick to hear . . ."

(MOM enters)

MOM   Charlie, I'm leaving and I . . . (want you)

CHARLIE   (Not listening) ". . . slow to speak . . ."

MOM   I need you to watch . . . (the)

(Interrupt)

CHARLIE   I'm not going to watch after my sister. She is so much trouble. All she ever wants to do is bug me.

MOM   Charlie, if you had waited to speak, you would have known I wanted you to watch the cookies in the oven, and help yourself to a warm one when the buzzer goes off. Your sister is over at a friend's house. (MOM leaves, saying): Good-bye now.

CHARLIE   Now what was that verse again? Let's see . . . "slow to speak and slow to anger."

SUSIE   (Comes in) Hi, Charlie.

CHARLIE   GET OFF MY BIBLE! YOU ARE MESSING IT UP! You are such a mess, you rub off on everything. If you don't get off my Bible, I'm going to give you a holy whack with it!

SUSIE   Boy, Charlie. You are really angry. You need to learn this neat verse I was going to tell you about this morning before you interrupted me. It's in James 1:19: "But let everyone be quick to hear, slow to speak and . . . (slow to anger).

(Interrupt)

CHARLIE   OH! I ALREADY KNOW THAT ONE! *(Leaves)*

SUSIE   He could have fooled me. Boys and girls, let's learn this verse together. Say the verse with me. James 1:19: "But let everyone be quick to hear, slow to speak and slow to anger." Charlie was memorizing this verse, but he wasn't obeying what it said. He was interrupting instead of listening, and he was losing his temper. Let's memorize this verse. But more important, let's obey it and be careful to listen and not get angry. Are you listening? *(Wait for response. If there is no response say again):* Are you listening? I can't hear you. *(Put nose in air.)* I smell smoke!

CHARLIE   *(Comes running across stage with fireman's hat on his head.)* Mom's cookies! I sure wish I had listened to Mom better when she told me to watch the cookies. Now I won't be able to eat them.

The Green-Eyed Monster

Characters

Girl puppet
Two boy puppets
Dad puppet

JOHN   Hey, Charlie, Susie, do you like my new bike? I worked really hard and saved a long time for it.

SUSIE   Wow, John, it looks really cool!

JOHN   What do you think, Charlie?

CHARLIE   Well, it's okay, I guess. I never really liked that color, and now most of the guys aren't buying that kind of bike anymore.

JOHN   Oh, well, I couldn't afford one of those real expensive bikes like some of the guys have, but I thought this one was pretty neat.

CHARLIE   Well, it's okay, John, but I'm going to wait and get one of the new super-cool bikes. I don't want to ride an out-of-style bike; but yours is all right.

JOHN   *(Dejected)* Well, I've got to be going. I was going to show Joe my new bike, but I think I'll just go home now. *(JOHN goes off.)*

SUSIE   Charlie, why did you do that to John?

CHARLIE   I didn't say anything bad about his dumb bike.

SUSIE   But you didn't say anything good, either. And, Charlie, I know you wanted a bike just like that one and that same color, too.

CHARLIE   Well, that was a long time ago. Who do you think you are, Miss Know-It-All? Why don't you go and ask John for a ride on his bike, if you like it that much. *(With a singing voice)* Susie likes John. Susie likes John.

SUSIE   Charlie, you're impossible.

(ALL puppets disappear. DAD and CHARLIE appear.)

DAD   Charlie, with the front door open earlier, I couldn't help but overhear what you said to John and Susie this morning.

CHARLIE   Well, Susie asked for it. She's always picking on me.

DAD   Charlie, I think you might have been jealous of John's new bike.

CHARLIE   Jealous! Not me! I don't care about that bike I've been wanting. *(Pause)* I mean about John's dumb bike.

DAD   See, Charlie. You might be a little jealous.

CHARLIE   (*Dejected*) Well, maybe a little.

DAD   Remember when the Whites got their new van just like the one we had been wanting?

CHARLIE   Yes, I remember.

DAD   Well, at first I was jealous, because we couldn't afford one and had to drive our old station wagon another couple of years.

CHARLIE   (*Surprised*) You were jealous?

DAD   Yes, Charlie, I was, but I remembered a verse we had just studied in Bible study, Romans 13:13: "Let us behave properly . . . not in strife and jealousy" (NASB).

CHARLIE   Then what did you do?

DAD   I obeyed this verse and went over to let Mr. White show me his new van. And you know what, Charlie?

CHARLIE   (*Excited*) What?

DAD   It was fun to see Mr. White so happy. Just because someone else is happy does not mean we need to be unhappy.

CHARLIE   I see your point, Dad. I didn't want John to be happy, because I couldn't have a new bike.

DAD   You got it, Charlie.

CHARLIE   That is probably why I was mean to Susie, too.

DAD   Most likely.

CHARLIE   I think I'll go find Susie and see if she wants to go to John's house to see if we can go riding with John. My bike still has lots of good miles left on it.

DAD   Sounds great!

After Church

Characters

Mom puppet
Dad puppet
Girl puppet
Boy puppet

Optional Prop

A tape with car noise

(Sit as in automobile. DAD and MOM in front, KIDS in back.)

SUSIE   Charlie! I couldn't believe the way you acted in church today! I could have just died!

CHARLIE   How was I to know you weren't supposed to raise your hand if you had to go to the bathroom? That's what we do at school.

MOM   Charlie, there are some things that are the same between school and church, but many things are different.

SUSIE   But Mom, Charlie embarrassed me so bad when he said, after the choir sang, "Boy, I never heard that commercial before."

DAD   Now Susie, Charlie has not been in church very much. He's still learning how to behave.

SUSIE   But Dad, when they were talking about the new budget, and Charlie asked why the pastor got paid so much when he only works one day a week, I could have just died!

MOM   Yes, Susie, but Charlie now realizes that the pastor works very hard all week, and not just on Sunday.

CHARLIE   Yes, I'm still learning. How was I supposed to know that I shouldn't put my marble in the offering plate? I didn't have any money and I thought God might like my best shooter.

DAD   Yes, Charlie, I know you meant well, but right now I think God wants you to keep your shooter. Maybe next week you can give some of the money you made collecting aluminum cans.

CHARLIE   That's a good idea. Dad, are you supposed to sleep in church? I noticed Susie sleeping, and she was drooling on her Bible.

SUSIE   Well . . . Well . . .

DAD   No, Charlie, we are not supposed to sleep in church.

CHARLIE   Why do we go to church, anyway?

MOM   We go to church to learn about God and to worship him.

CHARLIE   What does worship mean?

DAD   Worship is to tell God that we love him. That's why we sing and pray.

CHARLIE   Oh, I get it. We go to church to get something when we listen and learn, and to give to God when we worship.

DAD   Yes, Charlie, I think you're getting the true purpose of church.

MOM   One thing though, Charlie. Next Sunday don't ask the usher when recess is!

CHARLIE   Okay, Mom. I'll work on that next Sunday. I don't need a recess, anyway. I want to sit quietly and listen so I can learn a lot about God.

DAD   That's a good boy, Charlie. If you sit quietly you won't disturb others who are worshiping God.

SUSIE   Yeah! And I won't die of embarrassment. Dad and Mom, I'm sorry I slept during the sermon. I'm going to get to bed earlier next week so I can learn more about God, like Charlie.

DAD   It sounds like we are all going to do better in church next Sunday.

The Grass Is Always Greener

Characters

Dad puppet
Girl puppet
Boy puppet

(You can have CHARLIE sing this or read it dramatically. Do "soda pop" in echosound.)

CHARLIE:

    Oh, I wish I were a little soda pop
    (soda pop)
    Oh, I wish I were a little soda pop
    (soda pop)
    I'd go down with a slurp
      and up with a burp.
    Oh, I wish I were a little soda pop
    (soda pop).

(SUSIE comes up.)

CHARLIE   Hey, Susie, do you want to hear my new poem [song]?

SUSIE   Thanks, Charlie, but I heard you saying it [singing it] already.

CHARLIE   Susie, if you really could have anything or be anyone, who would you be?

SUSIE   Not a soda pop, that's for sure! Let me think. I think I would like to be a rich, famous, and beautiful movie star.

CHARLIE   I would like to be strong and handsome like Superman.

SUSIE   I'd like to look like Jenny. She has the prettiest hair, and her mom buys her anything she wants.

CHARLIE   Yes, I'd like to be Timmy. He always gets the neatest parts in the school play. His parents buy him acting lessons.

SUSIE   I'd like to be Amy. She never studies but makes good grades.

CHARLIE   I'd like to be like John. He runs so fast he beats everyone in our school.

SUSIE   I'd like to be Kristi. Her mom owns a clothes shop, and she gets all these *gorgeous (Say dramatically)* clothes.

CHARLIE   I'd like to be Paul. He has a motorcycle. That would be heaven! I sure wish I was someone rich.

DAD   Charlie, what did I hear you say? You want to be someone rich?

CHARLIE   Yes, sir. Susie and I were just thinking how nice it would be to be someone rich who could buy anything.

SUSIE   Don't worry, Dad, we'll buy you anything you want, too. How about a new ski boat?

CHARLIE   Yeah, Dad. What would make you happy?

DAD   Before I answer that question, Charlie and Susie, there are two verses from the Bible I would like you to listen to: Philippians 4:11 and 12. As you listen to me read them, see if you can tell me what it took to make Paul happy. He's the man who wrote these verses.

CHARLIE and SUSIE   Okay.

DAD   "I have learned how to get along happily whether I have much or little. I know how to live on almost nothing or with everything" (TLB). *(Pause.)* Okay, now, what did it take to make Paul happy?

CHARLIE   Well, this verse said he was happy when he didn't have very much.

SUSIE   But it also said he was happy when he had much or everything.

CHARLIE   I guess the answer is he was happy when he didn't have very much and when he did.

SUSIE   Well, that means he was happy all the time.

DAD   That's right, Susie. We learn from these verses that things like clothes and toys do not really make us happy. God wants people to learn to be happy with what they have.

SUSIE   I remember for my birthday how I just knew a wetsie doll should make me happy. All she did was get me wet. Now I don't even play with her anymore.

DAD   I thought when we finally were able to move into this house I would be happy. But you know, kids, I am just as happy as I was in our apartment.

CHARLIE   I see what you mean, Dad. Being happy is not because of things.

SUSIE   Carol, the richest girl in school, wrote a paper on being lonely and unhappy.

DAD   Let's remember to learn to be like Paul and be happy when we don't have very much and when we seem to have a lot. Then we will always be happy.

CHARLIE   I'm sure glad we had this talk. Susie and I were just leaving to go buy your Father's Day gift.

SUSIE   Now that we've had this talk we should be able to save some money.

DAD   I guess I get to practice what I preach.

CHARLIE   We're just teasing, Dad.

SUSIE   See you later.

DAD   Have fun and take your time shopping!

Night Monsters and Such

Characters

Girl puppet
Boy puppet

SUSIE   This is the day the Lord has made. I will be glad and rejoice in it. *I FEEL GREAT!*

CHARLIE   *(Come in, head hanging down, nightcap on head)* Why does everyone feel great around here except me? I feel awful!

SUSIE   What's wrong, Charlie, are you sick?

CHARLIE   Sick of not being able to sleep.

SUSIE   Why are you having trouble sleeping?

CHARLIE   It's all Mom's fault. I asked her to stay with me in my room, and she wouldn't.

SUSIE   Why not?

CHARLIE   She said she had to stay with Dad.

SUSIE   I didn't know Dad was chicken to stay by himself.

CHARLIE   Me neither.

SUSIE   Charlie, why do you want Mom to stay with you, anyway?

CHARLIE   I don't get afraid when she's in my room. After she says goodnight and leaves, I get scared and can't sleep.

SUSIE   Why are you afraid?

CHARLIE   I'm afraid that there is some monster in my closet or under my bed.

SUSIE   Charlie, there's no such thing as monsters. They're only pretend.

CHARLIE   I know that! They just seem like they're real.

SUSIE   Why don't you get Mom to look under your bed and in the closet before you go to sleep.

CHARLIE   I did, but that doesn't help. I guess I'm afraid to be by myself in the night.

SUSIE   Don't you remember the verse Dad read last night in family devotions?

CHARLIE   No, I was too busy trying to learn how to sleep with my eyes open.

SUSIE   It was in Psalm 4:8. It said, "In peace I will both lie down and sleep, for Thou alone, O LORD, dost make me to dwell in safety" (NASB).

CHARLIE   Wow! What a neat verse!

SUSIE   When I get afraid at night, sometimes it helps me to remember Jesus is always with his children and watching them.

CHARLIE That really helps, Susie. Thanks. I know I'll get a good night's sleep now that I know Jesus is with people even when it's dark.

SUSIE Why don't we ask Mom to write down that verse in Psalm 4:8 for us so we can put it up on our headboards.

CHARLIE That's a good idea. Maybe we'd better get her to write one for Dad, too.

SUSIE I'll get the paper and crayons.

CHARLIE I FEEL GREAT ALREADY!

Secret Servant

Characters

Boy puppet
Girl puppet

Props

Two small black masks for boy puppet (can be easily cut out of strip of black felt long enough to tie around the puppet's head)

Optional

Small black mask for each child in audience

CHARLIE *(Sneaking around with black mask on)*

SUSIE *(Comes up behind him and scares him)* Charlie, what are you doing?

CHARLIE I'm being a secret servant.

SUSIE A secret what?

CHARLIE A secret servant.

SUSIE What is that?

CHARLIE It's a person who does something nice for someone else and doesn't let them know who did it.

SUSIE Oh, that's why you're sneaking around.

CHARLIE Yes, I was going to leave this card with a verse on it and a note telling *(insert names of puppeteers)* I was praying for them.

SUSIE You're being a secret servant for them?

CHARLIE Yes.

SUSIE Why would you want to be a secret servant, anyway?

CHARLIE Jesus tells us in Matthew 20:26–28 that if we want to be great we are to be a servant of others. In verse 28 it says, "The Son of Man did not come to be served, but to serve" (NKJV). I'm a secret servant because I want to obey Jesus and be like him.

SUSIE Wow! That is neat! What verse are you giving to *(insert names of puppeteers)* this morning?

CHARLIE Luke 1:37: "With God nothing will be impossible."

SUSIE They told me that they had to work with a couple of dummies this morning.

SUSIE Hey! Wait a minute! They're working with us this morning!

CHARLIE I think I'll change this verse to one about loving others.

SUSIE That sounds good to me. Charlie, I would like to be a secret servant, too. I was reading this morning in 1 Thessalonians 5:11: "Encourage one another, and build up one another" (NASB). Being a secret servant would help me to be an encouragement to someone else.

CHARLIE   Let me get something for you (OPTIONAL: and for all these boys and girls) to remind you to do things for others.

SUSIE   Okay. *(As CHARLIE disappears)* Who was that masked man?

CHARLIE   Here's a mask for you, Susie.

SUSIE   Wow! Thanks, Charlie. I'm going to put this in my room to remind me to do nice things for others like Jesus.

OPTIONAL ENDING: *(Insert name of helper)* ————, could you come and pass out these masks for me? Boys and girls, these will remind you to be a secret servant, too.

Anger–Good or Bad?

Characters

Girl puppet
Boy puppet
Mom puppet
Dad puppet

CHARLIE   *(Angry)* Yes, you did!

SUSIE   *(Angry)* No, I didn't.

CHARLIE   If you don't tell me right away, I'll knock your block off!

SUSIE   Yeah, you and what army?

DAD   *(Firm)* Charlie, Susie, what are you two fighting about?

CHARLIE   Well, Dad, it's all Susie's fault, you see . . .

SUSIE   My fault! No way! If you wouldn't have . . .

DAD   Now Susie and Charlie, I don't think what you are fighting about is so important that you need to be yelling at each other.

(MOM enters.)

MOM   Yes, children, I could hear your loud voices all the way in the backyard.

DAD   Charlie and Susie, you need to learn to control your anger.

CHARLIE   But Dad, didn't Jesus get angry? We studied in Sunday school how Jesus got angry at the money changers in the Temple and drove them out, and he used a whip!

DAD   That's right, Charlie, Jesus did get angry, but that was different.

SUSIE   How was that different?

MOM   There are many different types of anger.

SUSIE   I don't understand.

DAD   Here's an example of good anger. Remember last year when Charlie was walking home from school, and he saw those two bullies beating up on little George?

SUSIE   Yes, I remember.

DAD   Remember how mad Charlie got and made those two boys stop picking on George?

CHARLIE   Boy, I was mad!

MOM   Well, that was good anger. Charlie saw a wrong being done and had a right to get angry and help George.

DAD   A good question to ask yourself before you get angry is, "Would Jesus be angry at this same thing?" If the answer is yes, then it is good anger.

MOM   Wrong anger comes when we are being selfish. Jesus never was angry to try to get his own way. He did just the opposite and stayed silent.

SUSIE   I guess we could all learn a lesson from Jesus.

CHARLIE   Yes, Susie and I were arguing because we both wanted our own way. That's the wrong kind of anger.

SUSIE   I see what you mean about good and bad anger. Now, Charlie, I'm sorry about our fight. It was my fault.

CHARLIE   No, Susie, it was my fault.

SUSIE   No, Charlie, it was really my fault.

CHARLIE   No, Susie, I mean it. It's my fault!

SUSIE   Listen here, meat head. I said it's my fault!

CHARLIE   You space cadet. If I said it's my fault, it's my fault.

SUSIE   Step outside, and I'll show you whose fault it is.

DAD   (Clears voice) Charlieee and Susieee . . .

CHARLIE   Okay, I see your point. Susie, you're right. It's all your fault.

SUSIE   All my fault?

CHARLIE   Okay, isn't that what you wanted?

SUSIE   Well, it's not *all* my fault!

MOM   Children, let's go upstairs and talk some more about anger. I think you need another reminder.

CHARLIE and SUSIE   (Looking at audience) Uh, oh!

CHARLIE   I sure wish I had learned my lesson about anger sooner.

SUSIE   Me, too! I think we won't forget this lesson.

CHARLIE   Every time we sit down today, we'll remember!

Truth or Consequences

Characters

Two boy puppets
Two girl puppets
Mom puppet

(CHARLIE and his friend JOHN WHITE come up. Have CHARLIE laughing and JOHN hanging his head.)

CHARLIE   Ha! Ha! John, I pulled one over on you.

JOHN   I trusted you at your word, Charlie.

CHARLIE   I had my fingers crossed, so my promise to help you mow and clean your yard after we did mine doesn't count.

JOHN   I don't know if I'll have enough time now to mow my own yard after spending my whole morning helping you.

CHARLIE   That's too bad, John. You should have paid more attention! Ha! Ha! Well, I'm going inside and watch T.V. See you later. *(CHARLIE goes off laughing.)*

JOHN   *(Goes off mumbling)* Crossed fingers . . .

(SUSIE and CHARLIE come up together.)

SUSIE   Charlie, the yard looks great.

CHARLIE   Thanks. John helped me.

SUSIE   How did you get John to help you?

CHARLIE   Why does it matter why he helped me? He just helped me.

SUSIE   He's some friend! John's sister Pam is coming over in a little while. I need to hurry and finish this dusting so we can play.

CHARLIE   Hey, if you'll go get me a Coke with lots of ice, I'll help you dust after I drink it.

SUSIE   That's great, Charlie. You're a terrific brother. *(Goes down)*

CHARLIE   I know! *(CHARLIE goes down.)*

SUSIE   *(Comes up)* Charlie, where are you? Are you finished with your Coke yet?

CHARLIE   *(Comes up)* Yes. Thanks, it was good.

SUSIE   Well, let me get you another dust rag.

CHARLIE   Oh! I'm not going to help you with the dusting. *(Laughing)*

SUSIE   Charlie, you promised!

CHARLIE   It doesn't count. I had my nostrils crossed!

SUSIE   Your nostrils crossed?

CHARLIE   That's right. You should have paid more attention. Ha! Ha!

43

SUSIE   Charlie, I trusted you. Now I won't be able to get done before Pam comes over.

CHARLIE   (Laughing as he leaves) There's a sucker born every minute.

SUSIE   Brothers! (SUSIE leaves.)

(Knocking sound. CHARLIE and PAM WHITE come up.)

CHARLIE   Hi, Pam. How are you doing?

PAM   Fine, Charlie. Is Susie here?

CHARLIE   I'll get her for you, if you'll go get the mail and newspaper for me.

PAM   Sure, Charlie. Thanks.

(PAM disappears for a minute, and CHARLIE stands there laughing.)

PAM   Here's your paper and mail, Charlie. Where's Susie?

CHARLIE   You can go find her. I had my tongue crossed so I didn't have to get her. (Laughing) You can go find her. (Goes off laughing and saying) Next time I'll use "My toes were crossed!" This is great!

PAM   Boys! (Goes off yelling.) Susie, Susie.

MOM   Charlie. Charlie.

CHARLIE   (Appears) Yes, Mom?

MOM   Charlie, I'm hearing some bad news about you.

CHARLIE   What about me?

MOM   I've been upstairs talking to Susie and Pam. They told me the tricks you played on both of them and on John this morning. You didn't do what you promised them.

CHARLIE   But Mom, I had my fingers, nostrils, and tongue crossed.

MOM   Charlie, that is an unfair trick. In my Bible study class at church this morning, we learned about this verse in Colossians 3:9 that says, "Do not lie to one another" (NKJV). Charlie, when you promise to help someone and you don't do what you promise, you are lying. It doesn't matter what you have crossed. You are to tell the truth and do what you say you will do.

CHARLIE   I surely haven't been doing that, have I?

MOM   No, son. People won't believe you anymore or help you if you continue to act this way and not do what you say or promise.

CHARLIE   I don't want them to do that.

MOM   Charlie, you need to tell Susie, Pam, and John you are sorry for not doing what you told them you would. Then you need to do something to make up to them the trouble you have caused them.

CHARLIE   Yes, Mom. I'll go upstairs and take Susie and Pam a Coke and finish dusting for Susie so they can go play. I could mow John's yard Friday because we are out of school and I can still do ours Saturday.

MOM   Good boy, Charlie. I'll take you at your word.

CHARLIE   I want people to be able to trust me. Mom, what's for dinner?

MOM   Liver and onions.

CHARLIE   There's no chance you have your ears crossed, is there?

MOM   No, son, but I made your favorite potatoes and dessert to go with it.

CHARLIE   Oh, boy, I'll hurry with the dusting!

MOM   Don't forget to call John, too.

CHARLIE   Okay. Bye, Mom.

Fresh Fragrance

Characters

Dad puppet
Mom puppet
Girl puppet
Boy puppet
Dog puppet

Prop

A clothespin for dog's nose

(MOM and DOG puppet come up together. The DOG has a clothespin on his nose.)

MOM   P.U. What is that smell? This is awful. Charlie, Charlie, where are you?

CHARLIE   I'm in here, Mom. *(CHARLIE comes up.)* What do you want? Yuck! What's that smell? It sure stinks in here.

MOM   I was hoping you could help me figure out what was causing this awful smell. You haven't been playing with your chemistry set again, have you?

CHARLIE   No, I let Bobby Brown borrow it for a few days.

MOM   I should call and warn Mrs. Brown that Bobby has your chemistry set.

CHARLIE   I'll go see if Susie knows what's causing this awful smell.

(CHARLIE disappears. DOG stays up.)

SUSIE   Gross! What's that smell? This is awful. How's a girl to breathe? I can see it now. Sweet young Susie Green dies from lack of fresh air. Film at eleven.

(Charlie returns.)

CHARLIE   There you are, Susie. I was looking for you. Is this awful smell because you are cooking dinner again?

SUSIE   No, Mom said we are eating at the Brown's home tonight.

CHARLIE   That's a relief. I was afraid we were having another one of your supper surprise dishes. The surprise is we live after we eat it. Ha! Ha!

MOM   *(Comes up behind.)* Charlie Green. That's no way to talk to your sister.

CHARLIE   Sorry, Mom. This smell has cut off the oxygen to my brain.

MOM   Maybe your dad knows what it is.

SUSIE   I bet he has his shoes off. Maybe that's this awful smell.

DAD   *(Appears)* I heard that, Susie.

SUSIE   Uh, oh. I'm sorry.

DAD   No, it's not my feet, but I have an idea. I saw Caleb chasing cats in the garbage dump on my way to work this morning.

EVERYONE   *(Looks at Caleb)* CALEB!! *(CALEB looks down.)*

SUSIE   How could you chase those nice cats? Serves you right. Now you'll have to have a bath.

CALEB   *(Whimpers and nudges up to Charlie.)*

CHARLIE   It's okay, Caleb, you were just doing what comes naturally to you. Susie, dogs chase cats.

CALEB   *(Nods head at Susie.)*

SUSIE   Take the dog's side. See if I care.

MOM   All right, children. Let's not fight.

DAD   This smell reminds me of a verse I read in the Bible this morning.

SUSIE   What verse could possibly remind you of this awful smell?

DAD   2 Corinthians 2:14 and 15. It says that our lives and actions should be like a pleasing fragrance so that others want to be around us and know more about Jesus.

CHARLIE   I see. When we act wrong or quarrel with others it's as if our lives smell rotten like Caleb here.

MOM   I think we all need to remember this verse. Thanks, Caleb, for helping us learn a good lesson.

SUSIE   Yes, thanks Caleb. Come on, Charlie. I'll help you give Caleb a bath.

(CALEB'S ears go up and he runs offstage.)

MOM   That's great, Susie.

DAD   Let's all work on being a pleasant fragrance of Christ when we go to the Brown's house for supper tonight.

MOM   That won't be too hard. Mrs. Brown just called. It seems they are taking us out for dinner. Bobby just smelled up their whole house.

CHARLIE   Oh, no! My chemistry set!

I'm Bored

Characters

Dad puppet
Girl puppet
Boy puppet

(SUSIE comes up. Yawns, looks disgusted, hangs head halfway over screen)

CHARLIE   Susie, you look unhappy. What's wrong?

SUSIE   I'mmmmmm boooorrrred!

CHARLIE   Why are you bored?

SUSIE   There's nothing to do around here. This place is boooooorrrring.

CHARLIE   Well, Susie, we could go for a ride on our bikes. Let's ride down to the park.

SUSIE   *(Quickly)* No, that's too boooorrrring.

CHARLIE   We could play the new video game I just got for my birthday. It's great fun.

SUSIE   *(Quickly)* No, that's too boooorrrring.

CHARLIE   We could go over to John and Pam's house and see if they want to go swimming at the pool.

SUSIE   *(Quickly)* No, swimming's boooorrrring. We can do that anytime.

CHARLIE   Susie, it seems no matter what I suggest you think it's boring.

SUSIE   That's not true. If you wanted to fly me to Hawaii, first class, of course, and we could stop off in Hollywood and I could star in a T.V. show, I would be excited about that suggestion. That's certainly not booooorrrring.

CHARLIE   Your expectations are too high!

DAD   What are you two talking about?

CHARLIE   Susie is bored, and I'm trying to give her ideas of what she could do, but she says everything I suggest is boring.

SUSIE   I can't help it, Dad. This place is soooo booooorrring. I can't stand it. I'd rather go to the dentist and have my teeth cleaned than stay around here!

DAD   You could clean your room or sweep the driveway.

SUSIE   Well, I guess I'm not *that* boooorrred.

DAD   Susie, you need to learn life is not always fun and exciting. We need to realize we should not always expect to be entertained.

SUSIE   I know I can't be having fun all the time. But what am I to do when I feel booorrred?

DAD   Well, one thing you could do is try to find something to do to help someone else.

SUSIE   You mean, like fumigate Charlie's room?

DAD   *(Firmly)* Now, Susie!

SUSIE   Sorry, Dad.

DAD   Susie, sometimes being bored is just being plain old selfish. We are just thinking of ourselves and need to think of others.

SUSIE   You mean when I'm booorrred, if I do something for someone else, I won't be bored anymore?

DAD   You're getting the idea. I think Galatians 6:10 might be a good verse for you. "So, then while we have opportunity, let us do good to all men, and especially to those who are of the household of the faith" (NASB).

SUSIE   I see your point, Dad. When I feel bored that means I have time that could be used as an opportunity to help others instead of only thinking about myself.

DAD   That's right, Susie. Life is not to be centered on us.

SUSIE   I think I'll go and help Mom weed the flower bed. Maybe I can help entertain her while she works instead of expecting you all to entertain me.

DAD   Good girl.

CHARLIE   Another crisis in the Green family solved! Now that's over, I'm kinda booorrrred myself.

DAD   Come on, Charlie. I've got a lawn mower that will keep you from being booooorrrrred.

CHARLIE   Oh, Dad. I was kidding.

DAD   I'm not.

Cheating

Characters

Girl puppet
Boy puppet

SUSIE   Charlie, what is that written on your hand?

CHARLIE   Oh, nothing.

SUSIE   Charlie Green, those words look like the spelling words we were tested on today.

CHARLIE   Well, er, uh (*Looks down at hands*). What do you know. I guess they are.

SUSIE   Charlie, don't you know that's cheating?

CHARLIE   But, Susie, I had to write them on my hand.

SUSIE   And why did you have to write them on your hand?

CHARLIE   Because Miss Jones changed the seating assignment. I sit next to John Brown now, and he writes so small I can't see the words anymore like when Cathy Johnson sat next to me.

SUSIE   You copied off of Cathy's paper?

CHARLIE   Well, not really. I just kind of checked my answers against her answers.

SUSIE   Charlie, that sounds like cheating to me!

CHARLIE   Cheating! I'm not cheating. I'm just saving time. We always get home from church late on Wednesday night, and I'm too tired to study for Thursday morning.

SUSIE   It sounds like you're making excuses. What about studying Wednesday afternoon when we get home from school?

CHARLIE   And miss my favorite show, "As the Puppets Turn?" No way!

SUSIE   Charlie, you're impossible.

CHARLIE   Which do you think God wants more? Me to miss Bible study to study for a spelling test or just to fudge a little on the test?

SUSIE   Charlie, you're not just fudging. You're cheating, and God wants you to go to church *and* study.

CHARLIE   It's no big deal. It's just a spelling test!

SUSIE   Do you remember the verse we studied last Wednesday night in Ephesians 4:28? It told us, "Let him who steals, steal no longer; but rather let him labor, performing with his own hands what is good" (NASB).

49

Charlie, when you cheat you are stealing someone else's work.

CHARLIE   You mean fudging on a test is stealing?

SUSIE   Yes, cheating on a test is sin.

CHARLIE   Wow, sin is serious!

SUSIE   Charlie, since I'm such a great sister and everything, I'll even get you some cookies while you study your spelling words.

CHARLIE   Since I'm not going to be fudging on my tests anymore, do you think I could have some of Mom's fudge?

SUSIE   I'll get you some fudge as long as it's the only fudge in your life.

CHARLIE   Thanks, Sis!

Bragging

Characters

Boy puppet
Girl puppet
Dad puppet
Mom puppet

SUSIE Oooh, Charlie, come here. You won't believe what happened to me today!

CHARLIE What happened to you, Susie?

SUSIE Well, as you might have expected, I won first place in our school track meet. But I'm sure you have heard already. I'm probably the talk of the whole town by now.

CHARLIE *(Mumbling)* Yes, I've heard a lot of people talking about you.

SUSIE What did you say?

CHARLIE *(More loudly)* I said, it's amazing what you can do!

SUSIE Yes, when God made me, he broke the runner's mold.

CHARLIE *(Mumbling)* There's always something for which to be thankful.

SUSIE What did you say?

CHARLIE *(More loudly)* With a sister like you, I wish I had four.

SUSIE Charlie Green, don't you wish you could be like me? I'm always the best

and the fastest, wherever I go. It must be hard to live in my shadow.

CHARLIE *(Mumbling)* I wish Dad would get his paddle!

SUSIE What did you say?

CHARLIE *(More loudly)* Yes, I'm just like a snail compared to you.

(MOM enters.)

SUSIE Hi, Mom! I just won the track meet AGAIN! Just call me Susie the Streak!

MOM I couldn't help but overhear you two talk. It sounded like you were bragging, Susie.

SUSIE But, Mom, I did win the track meet, and all I said was true!

MOM Yes, Susie, I know. But bragging is when you make yourself look big. It's better to let others speak well of you and not do it yourself. I have a verse I'd like to share with you. It's Proverbs 27:2: "Let another man praise you, and not your own mouth; a stranger, and not your own lips (NKJV)."

SUSIE You mean I shouldn't tell others about how great I am?

MOM It's fine to tell others about things you do, but let them decide if you're great or not.

SUSIE   I can tell others the facts but not try to make myself look good or them look bad.

MOM   I think you understand now, Susie.

CHARLIE   Yes, Susie. I might even tell the guys how well you did, but let me do it.

SUSIE   You know, Charlie, you're such a good brother, I'm tempted to brag about you at times. Oops, sorry!

MOM   It's okay to brag about others and to notice their improvements and accomplishments.

CHARLIE   I agree. It makes me want to do better when others notice something good I have done or accomplished.

MOM   Maybe if all of us would notice good things the others in our family were doing, we wouldn't have so much bragging around our house.

SUSIE   That sounds good. Let's try it.

DAD   Hi, family. I'm home.

MOM, CHARLIE and SUSIE   Hi, Dad.

CHARLIE   Welcome home, Dad. We sure appreciate you working hard all day.

SUSIE   Yes, Dad, you do such a good job at work and at home. I noticed how nice the new garden was coming along.

MOM   Honey, we're all proud of you. We're having some of your fresh vegetables for supper tonight.

DAD   I don't know what happened around here, but I sure hope it lasts. This is nice.

MOM   Proverbs 27:2 is what happened.

DAD   I'll have to find that verse later in my Bible. Susie, how did you do in your track meet today?

SUSIE   I won first place.

DAD   How great!

CHARLIE   Yes, we're going to call her Susie the Streak, now!

DAD   Let's all celebrate Susie the Streak's victory with ice cream cones tonight after supper.

EVERYONE   Yeah!

52

Forgive and Forget

Characters

Two girl puppets
Mom puppet

Optional Prop

Tape with sound of door slamming

(MOM up. Sound of door slamming optional. SUSIE comes up.)

SUSIE   I hate Pam White!

MOM   Susie, what in the world is wrong with you? Why are you talking this way?

SUSIE   Because I hate Pam White!

MOM   Calm down, Susie, and tell me what happened to cause you to say this about your best friend.

SUSIE   She's no longer my best friend. She's not even a friend!

MOM   Susie, take three deep breaths and tell me what happened.

SUSIE   *(Takes three very overexaggerated breaths)* Well, today at lunch, Pam asked me if I wanted to exchange my plain old peanutbutter-and-jelly sandwich for her meat sandwich. I said I would.

MOM   What's wrong with her offer?

SUSIE   She tricked me! Her sandwich was liverwurst, and I hate liverwurst! She started laughing and told me a trade was a trade and went to eat lunch with Jennifer.

MOM   It doesn't sound like Pam was being very nice today. Sometimes people just have a bad day and act mean. We all have been that way. We just have to learn to forgive each other. Susie, don't you think the best thing to do would be to forgive Pam?

SUSIE   Okay, I'll forgive her. I just hate her guts.

MOM   Susie, I think we need to have a talk about forgiveness. When you forgive someone you accept her again as a friend and forget about what she did.

SUSIE   You mean act like it never happened? You mean you don't make her pay by being mean back? That doesn't sound like any fun.

MOM   It's not, Susie, but that is what Jesus would want a person to do. It's hard to forgive sometimes.

SUSIE   But Mom, it seems she's always doing something like this. How many times do I have to forgive her?

MOM   The disciple, Peter, asked the same question. Listen to this verse and then tell me how many times you should forgive Pam. Matthew 18:21–22 says: "Then Peter came and said to Him, 'Lord, how often shall my brother sin against, me and I forgive him? Up to seven times?' Jesus said to him, 'I do not say to you up to seven times, but up to seventy times seven'" (NKJV).

SUSIE   Let's see, how much is seventy times seven? 490! We are to forgive 490 times? I'm going to keep track on my calendar of how many times Pam treats me mean, and when she gets to 490 times, I'm going to let her have it.

MOM   Wait a minute. I think you misunderstood this verse. Jesus is telling Peter to stop keeping track and to forgive. Susie, think of how many times Jesus has to forgive a person in a lifetime. If a person sinned just once a day and lived to be seventy, Jesus would have to forgive that person over twenty-five thousand times, and most people sin more than once a day!

SUSIE   Wow! If a person wants to be like Jesus she would have to forgive other people a lot, huh?

MOM   That's right, Susie. It's not always easy to do what Jesus says, but that is the best.

SUSIE   I understand, Mom. Do you think you could help me make some crafts tonight? Our Sunday school class is going to visit some people that can't get out of their houses because they are sick.

MOM   Sure, I'd be happy to help.

SUSIE   I think I'll call Pam and see if she wants to help.

MOM   Good girl. (Knocking sound) I'll get the door. (MOM disappears.) (PAM comes up.)

PAM   Susie, I'm sorry I was mean to you at school today.

SUSIE   Thanks, Pam. I've already forgiven you. Want to work on some crafts with me?

MOM   (Yelling from offstage) Pam, would you like to stay for dinner? We're having liverwurst casserole.

SUSIE and PAM   (Looking at each other) YUCK!! (Exit laughing)

T.V.

Characters

Dad puppet
Mom puppet
Boy puppet
Girl puppet
Grandpa puppet

Props

Cardboard box; sign that says "One Hour Later"

SCENE: CHARLIE staring at T.V. (cardboard box). Both turned sideways to audience.

DAD   *(Calling loudly from behind curtain)* Chaarlie! Chaarlie!

CHARLIE   *(Makes no reply.)*

(DAD appears.)

DAD   Charlie! Why didn't you answer me? Didn't you hear me?

CHARLIE   *(Still staring at T.V.)* Yes, Dad, I heard you, but I've only got five minutes left of "As My Stomach Churns."

DAD   Well, okay, but as soon as your show is over I'd like your help in the garage, please.

CHARLIE   *(Still staring at T.V.)* Sure Dad, I'll be right there.

(DAD goes offstage.)

(SIGN comes up stating One Hour Later.)

GRANDPA   *(Offstage)* Charlie, Charlie!

(GRANDPA appears.)

GRANDPA   Charlie, your father was wondering what happened to you. He needs your help.

CHARLIE   *(Staring at T.V.)* Oh, sure, I'll be right there.

(GRANDPA goes offstage.)

(SIGN comes up stating One Hour Later.)

SUSIE   *(Calling from offstage):* Chaarlie, Chaarlie!

(SUSIE appears.)

SUSIE   Charlie Green, Dad is looking for you and he does not sound too happy. I'd come if I were you.

CHARLIE   *(Still starring at T.V.)* Yes, sure; be right there.

DAD, GRANDPA, and SUSIE   *(Offstage)* Chaarlie, Chaarlie!

(DAD, GRANDPA and SUSIE all appear.)

DAD   *(Sternly)* Charlie Green, where have you been? I've been trying to get you to help for hours!

(CHARLIE turns and looks at them.)

SUSIE   *(Angrily)* Yes, Charlie, I had to help . . . *(raising voice)* and I broke a nail!

DAD   Charlie, I have needed your help, and you never came.

CHARLIE   *(Sheepishly)* Well, after I finished watching "As My Stomach Churns," they showed previews of "Wheel of the Misfortunate," and I had to see if the plumber from New York won the new car; and then it was time for "The Cartoon Marathon," which is my absolute favorite; and then . . .

DAD   *(Interrupts)* Charlie, you've been watching T.V. all this time?

CHARLIE   *(Hangs head)* Yes, Dad, I guess I was watching T.V. all the time.

GRANDPA   It sounds like T.V. has become an idol to you.

SUSIE   *(Shaking head vigorously)* Yes, Charlie, an idol! *(Turns to Grandpa)* Grandpa, what's an idol?

GRANDPA   An idol is anything which keeps people away from God; or from doing what God would want them to do.

CHARLIE   I remember hearing about an idol in Sunday school, but our teacher said it was something like a statue which people bowed down to and thought was a god.

GRANDPA   That's true, Charlie, and in many places around the world, even today, people still bow to idols.

SUSIE   Gosh, that's terrible.

CHARLIE   But, Grandpa, I don't understand how T.V. can be an idol.

GRANDPA   Well, T.V. is not bad in itself. It is okay to watch some good shows and sports, but when it causes you to waste time or not be obedient—let's say to your father—it becomes just like an idol.

DAD   Yes, Charlie, Grandpa is right. You were watching too much T.V., and it was causing you to be disobedient, and you wasted your whole afternoon.

CHARLIE   I'm sorry, Dad. I didn't realize I was doing wrong by watching too much T.V.

GRANDPA   A Bible verse which could help is 1 Corinthians 6:12: "All things are lawful for me, but not all things are profitable. All things are lawful for me, but I will not be mastered by anything" (NASB). We have to be careful not to let T.V. become our master. Sometimes I'm tempted to watch too much T.V., too.

CHARLIE   I'm glad to hear I'm not the only one who has this problem.

DAD   Charlie, you need to do something nice for Susie. She did more than her share of the work today.

CHARLIE   Okay, Dad. Susie, I won't trip you for at least one week.

DAD   That's not exactly what I had in mind.

CHARLIE   I'll take your turn doing the dishes for this next week.

MOM   *(Appears)* Here all of you are. I've been looking everywhere for someone to go and help me do the grocery shopping.

CHARLIE   Sorry, Mom. My absolute, all-time, forever favorite T.V. show is just starting.

DAD, GRANDPA, and SUSIE   Charlie would love to go!

CHARLIE   Right! No more idols for me. I'd be happy to go.

DAD   Good boy, Charlie, you're learning.

GRANDPA   By the way, Charlie, what is your absolute, all-time, forever favorite T.V. show?

CHARLIE   "Charlie's Angels" reruns, of course!

Responsibility

Characters

Dog puppet
Cat puppet
Boy puppet
Girl puppet
Mom puppet

Props

Dog dish and cat dish; signs that say "Next Morning" and "That Night"

(DOG puppet comes partially up and hangs head down.)

MOM   Good morning, Caleb.

CALEB   *(Whimpers)*

MOM   What's wrong, Caleb? *(If your dog has a paw, attach an empty dish to his paw and hang over now; or if your dog does not have a paw, hang over next to the dog on a line attached to a stick. It's fun to have a little saying on the bottom of the dish, like "Feed the Dog" or "Dog Starving".)*

MOM   Did Charlie forget to feed you last night?

CALEB   *(Nods yes)*

MOM   Charlie, come here, please.

CHARLIE   Good morning, Mom. Did you call me?

CALEB   *(Looks up with hope)*

MOM   Yes, son. Did you forget to feed Caleb last night?

CHARLIE   I didn't have *time* to feed him.

MOM   Son, you need to feed Caleb now. Look at the poor dog. He's starving.

CALEB   *(Sinks down even lower)*

CHARLIE   But, Mom, I'll be late for school.

MOM   Charlie, you have to learn responsibility. I remember a young man who only a few months ago promised to take care of the dog all by himself if we let him get a dog.

CHARLIE   Okay, Mom, I'll feed him. Come here, Caleb.

(ALL leave. Show sign Next Morning. CAT hangs its head with empty dish. Write on bottom of dish again.)

MOM   Susie, come here, please.

SUSIE   Yes, Mom.

MOM   Did you feed Methuselah last night?

SUSIE   No, Mom, I didn't think it would hurt him to miss *one* meal. I just didn't have time. *(METHUSELAH hangs head.)*

MOM   Susie, you need to learn responsibility for your animal.

SUSIE   Okay, Mom. Come here, Methuselah. *(ALL leave.)*

(Show sign Next Morning again. Both CALEB and METHUSELAH are hanging their heads with their dishes.)

MOM Poor doggie and kitty. You are starving again. *(DOG and CAT nod yes.)*

MOM Come here, you two. I'll feed you since the kids are gone for school already. We need to teach Charlie and Susie a lesson. *(CALEB and METHUSELAH bark and meow in agreement.)*

MOM I have an idea. We'll try it tonight. *(ALL leave.)*

(Pause, Sign: That Night. MOM, CHARLIE, and CALEB come up.)

CHARLIE Hi, Mom! What's for supper? I'm starved!

MOM Charlie, I didn't have *time* to make supper tonight. You can just wait to eat until breakfast.

CHARLIE You didn't have time?

MOM Yes, son. I was too busy feeding and taking care of Caleb today.

CALEB *(Woofs; rubs against MOM and pants.)*

CHARLIE Uh oh, I didn't feed Caleb this morning. I ran out of *time*.

MOM I had to take care of your responsibilities and I didn't have *time* to take care of my responsibility to make supper.

(SUSIE and METHUSELAH appear.)

SUSIE What's for dinner, Mom? I'm ready to eat.

MOM Susie, I thought you wouldn't mind missing *one* meal, so I decided not to make supper tonight. You can wait until breakfast to eat.

METHUSELAH *(Meows)*

MOM That's right, Methuselah. He had to go without supper last night, when you said it wouldn't matter if he missed just one meal.

CHARLIE and SUSIE But, Mom, we're hungry.

MOM Charlie and Susie, we all have responsibilities in our family. When one of us doesn't do our part, things don't run smoothly. Neither of you have been taking care of your responsibilities.

SUSIE I think I understand what you mean, Mom. I'm sorry I've been neglecting my responsibilities of taking care of Methuselah. I'll do better. One meal *is* important.

METHUSELAH *(Rubs up against Susie and purrs.)*

CHARLIE I need to set my alarm five minutes earlier so I have time to take care of my responsibilities to Caleb.

CALEB *(Barks)*

MOM Okay, children, I think you have learned your lessons. I'll go make us all hot dogs.

EVERYONE Yea! *(CALEB barks, METHUSELAH meows.)*

MOM Just remember, one of my responsibilities as a mother is to teach you children responsibility. Next time we *will* do without supper.

SUSIE Don't worry, Mom, we've learned our lesson.

CHARLIE Mom, since you had to do our chores this morning, we'll help you with supper now and then do our homework after dinner.

MOM Good, kids. I think the Green family is running smoothly again.

SUSIE Let's get some *fuel* to keep us running smoothly.

METHUSELAH Meow!

SUSIE Okay, no more jokes!

Partiality

Characters

Girl puppet
Mom puppet

Props

Pencil; small piece of tape. Tape pencil to Susie's right hand.

SUSIE   (Hands behind screen: move her right hand and head as if she is writing and reading.)

MOM   Susie, you surely look busy. What could be so important to get you up this early?

SUSIE   (Put hand over now with pencil.) I'm writing a letter to Grandpa and Grandma Smith.

MOM   How sweet of you. I'm sure my dad and mom will enjoy getting a letter from you. I know they get lonely with all of us living so far away.

SUSIE   I wish they lived closer.

MOM   Me, too. Well, we can be thankful we have Grandpa and Grandma Green right here in our city of Greenville.

SUSIE   I'd rather have Grandpa and Grandma Smith live here.

MOM   Why do you say that, Susie?

SUSIE   Well, Grandpa and Grandma Smith have more money and give us prettier presents. That's why I'm writing them this letter. It's my birthday next week, and I want a Burpsie Wetsie Doll like Pam's. I know Grandpa and Grandma Green can't get me one, so I thought I would write Grandpa and Grandma Smith.

MOM   I'm disappointed in your actions. It sounds to me like you're being selfish with your love.

SUSIE   Not really, Mom. I have plenty of love for Grandpa and Grandma Smith.

MOM   Susie, that's only because of what they do for you.

SUSIE   Why's that wrong?

MOM   The Bible tells us, in James 2:9, that when we treat someone differently because they have more money or can do more for us, it is showing partiality.

SUSIE   What's partiality?

MOM   Do you remember the other day when you were telling me how hurt you felt because your teacher at school treats Charlotte better than everyone else?

SUSIE   Yes. She's always the teacher's favorite because she's the principal's daughter.

MOM   That's showing partiality. Listen to this verse in James 2:9 and then tell me what showing partiality is called. "But if you show partiality, you commit sin" (NKJV).

SUSIE   Uh oh! It's a sin.

MOM   That's right; showing partiality is sin. This whole first part of James chapter 2, is about a person who lets a rich man have the best place at the table and makes a poor man stand or sit on the floor.

SUSIE   How mean.

MOM   That's right. It is mean.

SUSIE   I can see what you're saying, Mom. I'm being wrong when I like Grandpa and Grandma Smith more than Grandpa and Grandma Green because they can do more for me.

MOM   Good girl, Susie. God made each of us to be different, but we are all special to him. It's wrong to choose some people over others. We need to appreciate each person.

SUSIE   That's right. Who would help me with my math homework if Grandpa Green moved away?

MOM   Surely not me!

SUSIE   I was being selfish. I think I'll make some cookies and take them over to Grandpa and Grandma Green today. Don't worry, Mom, I'm not showing any partiality. I'll write Grandpa and Grandma Smith a letter and won't even mention my birthday.

(SUSIE leaves.)

MOM   *(Looks at audience)* Oh, dear, with the cookies *she* makes, I think she doesn't realize she is showing partiality to Grandpa and Grandma Smith by only sending them a letter. I'd better go make sure the fire extinguisher is working!

Big Ears, Eyes, and Mouth

Characters

   Girl puppet
   Boy puppet
   Mom puppet
   Dad puppet

Prop

   Boy puppet with big, overexaggerated bandage on ear.

CHARLIE   Susie, oh Susie . . .

SUSIE   What do you want, Charlie?

CHARLIE   I know who you like.

SUSIE   No you don't.

CHARLIE   You like Sylvester Day.

SUSIE   Charlie, how did you find out?

CHARLIE   *(in a sing-song voice)* Susie loves Sylvester. Susie loves Sylvester. Susie loves Sylvester.

SUSIE   Charlie, stop it. Stop teasing me.

CHARLIE   Okay, I won't say that anymore.

SUSIE   *(Sighs)* That's a relief.

CHARLIE   Susie and Sylvester up in a tree, k-i-s-s-i-n-g . . .

SUSIE   *(Interrupts)* S-s-s-h, Charlie, someone will hear you, and then Sylvester will find out.

CHARLIE   *(A little louder)* Susie and Sylvester up in a tree k-i-s-s-i-n-g. First comes love, then comes marriage; then comes Susie with a baby carriage.

SUSIE   *(Yells)* Mom . . . Mom . . . make Charlie stop.

MOM   Charlie, what are you doing? Are you aggravating your sister?

CHARLIE   No, I'm just telling the truth.

SUSIE   Mom, please make him stop.

CHARLIE   What's wrong, Susie? You afraid I'll tell Sylvester you like him?

SUSIE   Charlie, quit! *(Loudly)* Mom!

MOM   All right, children, that's enough.

SUSIE   Charlie, how did you find out I like Sylvester? I haven't even told my best friend, Pam, yet. I just wrote it in my *(Pause for effect)* DIARY. Charlie, you've been reading my diary? MOM!

MOM   Charlie, is that true? Were you reading your sister's diary?

CHARLIE   Well, yes, but she shouldn't leave it lying around if she doesn't want anyone to read it.

SUSIE   I didn't leave it lying around.

CHARLIE   Yes, you did. It was lying under your bed in a box under your winter sweaters.

MOM   Charlie, that is not leaving it lying around! You were snooping.

DAD   *(Comes up)* What is this? Charlie, are you snooping around again?

MOM   I thought you would have learned your lesson yesterday from your fall when I opened the door and you had been listening to Dad and me with the glass to your ear.

CHARLIE   *(Rubs ear with bandage)* That still hurts.

DAD   Son, I think you need to learn to respect other people's privacy.

CHARLIE   I was just practicing this week's memory verse from Sunday school. Proverbs 10:14 says, "Wise people store up knowledge" (NKJV). And, boy, have I stored up some great knowledge!

DAD   That is not what this verse is teaching.

MOM   Charlie, why do you want to learn this knowledge? You are working so hard at finding out about other people.

CHARLIE   So I can tell others, and they will think I know a lot.

DAD   Do you think telling other people personal things hurts the person the story is about?

CHARLIE   Well, yes, I guess so.

SUSIE   Dad, you're right. I was really hurt when Charlie was going to tell others I like Sylvester.

DAD   What did the rest of your verse in Proverbs 10:14 say, Charlie?

CHARLIE   "Wise people store up knowledge, but the mouth of the foolish is near destruction" (NKJV).

MOM   Charlie, when you share other people's personal thoughts that were meant to be private, you bring destruction, just as this verse says. And, according to this verse, you are a fool.

CHARLIE   I don't want to be a fool.

DAD   Five verses later, in the same chapter in Proverbs, it says, "He who restrains his lips is wise" (v. 19 NKJV).

CHARLIE   I want to be wise.

MOM   Charlie, when you go around spending your time finding out other people's private feelings, it's harder to restrain your lips. That means to keep quiet.

CHARLIE   You're right, Mom. It's hard not to tell everyone.

DAD   It's better we don't find out everything. Do you understand?

CHARLIE   Yes.

SUSIE   Mom, I'm going to call Pam. *(Leaves.)*

MOM   Okay. *(CHARLIE starts to run off.)*

DAD   Charlie, where are you going in such a hurry?

CHARLIE   To listen on the extension phone.

MOM   Do you think that is *wise?*

CHARLIE   No, you're right. That's what a fool would do, and I don't want to be a fool.

DAD   Good boy, Charlie. I think you learned a good lesson.

CHARLIE   Now that I'm not going to be snooping around anymore, I'm going to have a lot of free time.

DAD   Good. You can come help me clean up the garage.

CHARLIE   Me and my *big* mouth!

Forgetting Failure

Characters

Girl puppet
Boy puppet
Mom puppet
Cat puppet

CHARLIE *(Muttering):* I hate myself. I always seem to do the wrong things. No wonder nobody likes me.

SUSIE Charlie, Charlie, you are in MAJOR TROUBLE now!

CHARLIE I believe it. What did I do now?

SUSIE Well, you put Mom's favorite plant on the windowsill this morning, and now it's broken on the floor.

CHARLIE Oh, no!

SUSIE *(Sing-song voice)* Charlie's in major trouble; Charlie's in major trouble. Ha! Ha! I'm gonna tell, and Charlie's gonna be in major trouble.

CHARLIE I can't seem to do anything right. I hate myself.

MOM Charlie, you shouldn't talk about yourself that way. What's causing you to feel this way about yourself?

CHARLIE Well, you see, Mom . . .

SUSIE Charlie broke your favorite potted plant.

MOM How did this happen?

SUSIE Charlie's in major trouble, huh, Mom?

MOM Susie, you are going to be in major trouble if you don't let your brother explain.

CHARLIE Well, Mom, this morning I noticed your plant wasn't looking very good, so I watered it and put it on the windowsill to get some sun. Now it's broken on the floor.

MOM Charlie, this is not your fault.

CHARLIE It seems everything I do is wrong.

MOM Son, you did a good thing in trying to help my plant. I appreciate your help. It was just an accident. You had no way of knowing my plant would fall.

SUSIE You mean Charlie's not in major trouble?

MOM No, Susie, he's not even in minor trouble.

SUSIE Shucks!

MOM Charlie, you shouldn't be so hard on yourself.

CHARLIE It seems I make so many mistakes and I try to be good.

MOM Honey, we all make mistakes. I was reading in my devotions this morning what Paul said in Romans 7:15: "I am not practicing what I would like to do, but I am doing the very thing I hate" (NKJV).

CHARLIE   You mean Paul, the great apostle, made mistakes?

MOM   Yes, and you know, Paul also told us how to handle our mistakes and failures, in Philippians 3:13 and 14.

CHARLIE   How?

MOM   We are to forget them, press on, and try to do better. Learn from our mistakes and then forget them.

CHARLIE   I'm encouraged, Mom. We all make mistakes. Even Paul!

MOM   Charlie, how many times have you said bad things about yourself like what I just heard?

CHARLIE   Quite a few times.

MOM   Before dinner I want you to write down for me ten things that you have done a good job on this week, and we'll thank God for helping you do these *good* things during our supper devotions.

CHARLIE   Boy, that's going to be hard.

MOM   Now Charlie, remember, don't be so hard on yourself.

CHARLIE   Okay, Mom.

MOM   That's all I can ask. *(METHUSALEH the cat comes up.)* Hi, Methuselah kitty. What are you doing in the house?

CHARLIE   I guess Susie forgot to put the cat out this morning.

MOM   That's how my favorite plant got knocked down. Methuselah jumped up on the windowsill. *(Turns toward Susie)* Susie, you are in MAJOR TROUBLE!

SUSIE   There's no chance we can forget this mistake, is there, Mom?

MOM   No, Susie. First, you need to learn from this mistake.

CHARLIE   Uh, oh. Mom's headed for the paddle. This is the third time this week Susie has been warned about putting Methusaleh out. I think Susie's going to have a hard time forgetting what lies "behind" her for a little while!

Exaggeration

Characters

Boy puppet
Girl puppet
Dad puppet
Mom puppet
Grandpa puppet

CHARLIE *(Excited)* Susie! Susie! You won't believe it! I caught a ten-pound fish on the campout this weekend! It took two of us to get him in!

SUSIE *(Appears)* What did you say, Charlie? How big was your fish?

CHARLIE It was ten pounds!

SUSIE Wow, that's great! A ten-pound fish! *(SUSIE disappears.)*

CHARLIE *(Excited)* Dad! Dad! I caught a fifteen-pound fish on the campout this weekend.

DAD *(Appears)* Charlie, I can't believe it! You caught a fifteen-pound fish? That must be close to a record! *(DAD disappears.)*

CHARLIE *(Excited)* Mom! Mom! *(MOM appears.)* I caught a twenty-pound fish on the campout this weekend, and it took four of us to get him on shore!

MOM Charlie, that's wonderful! I've never heard of a fish that big being taken out of Lake Greenville!

CHARLIE Dad said it was probably a state or even a national record! *(DAD and SUSIE appear.)*

DAD and SUSIE How big did you say your fish was?

CHARLIE Er, ah, um . . . it was about . . . well almost . . . It was really big!

DAD and SUSIE How many people did it take to land your fish?

CHARLIE Well . . . uh . . . er . . . ah . . . John handed me the net, and Billy and Joe cheered as I brought him in, so it was kind of like four of us.

DAD It sounds like you are exaggerating. And did I really say your fish was a state or national record?

CHARLIE *(Slowly)* Well, no not exactly, but it could be.

DAD Yes, Charlie, it could be, but I didn't say it was a record.

CHARLIE What is exaggeration exactly?

DAD Exaggeration is when you tell a story that is true but make it sound bigger and better than it really was.

MOM Exaggeration is a sin, because when you exaggerate you are not telling the truth, but you are lying.

CHARLIE Lying! Gosh, I'm sorry. I didn't mean to lie.

DAD   Yes, Charlie, you need to be careful. You can tell an exciting story, but don't stretch truth.

MOM   Remember what God tells us in the Bible in 1 Kings 2:4: "Walk before Me in truth with all [your] heart" (NKJV).

CHARLIE   Mom, I do want to follow God and do what is right.

GRANDPA   *(Enters excited)* Charlie, I just heard you caught a whale in Lake Greenville. I think we will call you Jonah.

CHARLIE   Well, Grandpa, it wasn't a whale, but he did weigh three pounds, and we did have a *whale* of a good time!

DAD   That's good, Charlie. Now people can always trust in you and believe what you say is true.

CHARLIE   I'm going to work on my exaggeration. Mom, what's for dinner?

MOM   Fish, of course!

CHARLIE   Very funny, Mom.

DAD   Speaking of Jonah reminds me: Do you know what the whale said? "You can't keep a good man down."

GRANDPA   *(Pushes DAD down behind curtain)* Are you sure you can't keep a good man down?

MOM and CHARLIE   *(Laughing)* Good job, Grandpa!

Cliques

Characters

Girl puppet
Boy puppet
Mom puppet

Optional Prop (depending on your location)

We use a smoke bomb to have smoke come up from behind the curtain. One is very inexpensive. We light it ten seconds before we want smoke and put it in a big gallon tin can. We buy the smoke bombs at the fireworks stands around the fourth of July.

SUSIE   Charlie, Jennifer is coming over to play in about an hour.

CHARLIE   Jennifer? You just told me yesterday you don't like Jennifer.

SUSIE   I didn't like her yesterday when I had Pam to play with. But she's okay today, because Pam's gone to her grandma's and there's no one else to play with.

CHARLIE   Girls! I'll never figure you out. It seems you can only play with one other person. What's wrong with playing with three?

SUSIE   *(Defensively)* That's not true, Mr. Know-It-All.

CHARLIE   Well, Bobby and I are both going over to play with Steve today.

SUSIE   You mean the new boy down the street?

CHARLIE   He's the one!

SUSIE   You told me you didn't like him yesterday.

CHARLIE   That was yesterday, before I found out what neat toys he has. His dad's a toy salesman.

SUSIE   Boys! I'll never figure you out. It seems you only like the person who can benefit you the most.

MOM   *(Comes up)* Good morning, kids! What are you all going to do this beautiful day?

SUSIE   I've invited Jennifer to come over and play.

CHARLIE   Bobby and I are going over to play with the new boy down the street.

MOM   Great! You can have some of the cookies I am making to share with your friends. They're chocolate chip!

SUSIE   That's what smells so great!

CHARLIE   Chocolate chip! My favorite!

MOM   I want you kids to know how proud I am of you both.

SUSIE   Why, Mom?

MOM   Susie, I'm proud of you for inviting Jennifer over to play. I noticed at church she's often sitting by herself. It's sweet of you to be her friend. *(SUSIE starts hanging her head lower and lower.)* She must be lonely, and to see you being nice to her makes me proud of you.

SUSIE   *(Mumbling)* Thanks, Mom.

MOM   Charlie, I am thrilled you and Bobby are playing with the new boy on the street and making him feel welcome. *(CHARLIE starts hanging his head lower and lower.)* It's probably hard moving to a new place. You kids just make me feel so proud.

CHARLIE   Nothing to it, Mom.

MOM   I was studying for my Bible study class and reading John 13:34. Listen to the Lord's command: "A new commandment I give to you . . . that you also love one another" (NKJV). It would be easy for you, and Bobby to just play alone, but you are including Steve. Susie, it would be easy for you to just play with Pam, but you're not. You both are showing love and not being selfish. As this verse says, people are to love others like Jesus did.

CHARLIE   Mom, I have to tell you something.

SUSIE   Me, too.

CHARLIE   We were being selfish with our love today.

SUSIE   We both were being nice to Jennifer and Steve for selfish reasons.

CHARLIE   But I'm going to change my reasons now that I understand Jesus wants people to love everyone.

SUSIE   Me, too. I'm not going to be selfish with my love.

MOM   I'm glad you kids told me. We'll all work on loving others, not just the ones who are easy to love.

SUSIE   Mom, would it be okay for me to offer Jennifer a ride to church with Pam and me on Sunday?

MOM   Sure.

CHARLIE   We might have to get a bus, Mom.

MOM   Why's that, Charlie?

CHARLIE   I was just going to ask if I could invite Steve.

MOM   We'll take two trips, if necessary.

CHARLIE   What's that smell?

SUSIE   Why is there smoke coming out of the kitchen?

MOM   My cookies!

CHARLIE and SUSIE   That's okay, Mom. We still *Love* you!

Heaven Is a Wonderful Place for a Little Later

Characters

Girl puppet
Boy puppet
Dad puppet
Grandpa puppet

(DAD, CHARLIE, and SUSIE come up.)

SUSIE   Dad, I was so embarrassed this morning in Sunday school.

DAD   Why, Susie?

SUSIE   Our lesson this morning was on heaven, and the teacher asked how many of us wanted to go to heaven.

DAD   What's so embarrassing about that?

SUSIE   Well, everyone raised their hand except Charlie. I was so embarrassed.

DAD   Charlie, why didn't you raise your hand?

CHARLIE   I thought the teacher was getting up a group to go to heaven right then, and I want to wait a while.

SUSIE   Charlie, she was talking about going to heaven when a person dies.

CHARLIE   I know that now.

GRANDPA   *(Comes up)* Did I hear someone mention heaven?

DAD   Yes, Dad, the kids and I were just talking about heaven.

SUSIE   Charlie didn't raise his hand today in Sunday school when the teacher asked us who wanted to go to heaven, because he thought she was leaving right then.

GRANDPA   Don't feel badly, Charlie. People are a little afraid because heaven is something new, and we're afraid of new and different things sometimes.

SUSIE   But Grandpa, our teacher said heaven is a wonderful place. There will be no crying.

GRANDPA   You're right, Susie. The Bible describes heaven in Revelation 21:3–4. It says, "God Himself shall be among them, and He shall wipe away every tear from their eyes; and there shall no longer be any death; there shall no longer be any mourning, or crying, or pain" (NASB).

CHARLIE   No more pain. How wonderful!

GRANDPA   That surely is true. The other day I chipped my tooth on a seedless grape! Whenever I bend over now to get something, I check to make sure my shoelaces are tied and do everything I can while I'm down there, because it's so hard to get up and down anymore. It will be nice for people to kneel at God's throne and not have to worry about creaking when they get up and down! The older a person gets the more he looks forward to heaven and no more pain.

SUSIE   Heaven also sounds pretty with pearl gates and all those pretty, bright, shining jewels. But the best part is Jesus is in heaven.

DAD   When a person knows Jesus as her Savior, it's like going home.

SUSIE   Our teacher told us Jesus is building mansions for his followers.

CHARLIE   You mean a person gets a mansion when he goes to heaven?

SUSIE   Yes, prepared by Jesus.

CHARLIE   Wow! All this talk about heaven makes it not seem so scary. I hope our teacher talks about heaven more next week.

DAD   We'll read about it tonight in Revelation 20 and 22 from the Bible before you go to bed.

CHARLIE   Wow, I can't wait for bedtime!

DAD   Hold me up! That's a first! Charlie looking forward to bed!

GRANDPA   Charlie, there will be no bedtimes in heaven, because there is no night and day.

CHARLIE   Heaven sounds perfect. When my teacher asks us to raise our hands if we want to go to heaven, I'm going to raise both of mine!

Being Courteous

Characters

Boy puppet
Girl puppet
Dad puppet
Grandpa puppet
Grandma puppet
Dog puppet

Props

Tape player and music cassette.

SCENE: *Music playing very loudly.*

CHARLIE   (*Appears singing to the music*)

SUSIE   (*Calls from behind curtain*) Chaaar-rrlie! Chaaarrrlie!

(*Music goes off. CALEB is howling.*)

SUSIE   (*Appears*) Charlie Green! You are going to break the windows in our neighbor's house if you don't turn that music down!

CHARLIE   What's wrong? Don't you like my new tape?

(*CALEB stops howling.*)

SUSIE   It's not whether I like your music or not, it's just too loud!

CHARLIE   You're just being too picky. I had my door closed!

(*Dad and GRANDPA appear.*)

DAD   What was that noise? Two pictures just fell off the wall downstairs.

GRANDPA   My, my, was that a sonic boom I heard?

(*GRANDMA appears.*)

DAD   Hello, Grandma.

GRANDMA   What?

DAD   I said, "Hello, Grandma."

GRANDMA   What? I can't hear you! Some loud noise just broke my hearing aid.

(*CALEB starts to howl behind the stage.*)

CHARLIE   Oops, sorry! I guess I was playing my new tape a bit too loudly.

SUSIE   A little? Any more loudly and Caleb would have left home.

(*CALEB appears, rubbing his ears with his paw.*)

CALEB   (*Looking at CHARLIE*) Woof! Woof!

DAD   Charlie, you need to be more courteous with things like loud music.

CHARLIE   I guess so, Dad. I didn't want to bother anyone. I just wanted to play my music good and loud.

(Baby starts crying in the background.)

GRANDPA   Uh,oh, it sounds like the new baby next door is crying. I guess she woke up from her nap.

CHARLIE   It sounds like everybody ended up listening to my tape.

SUSIE   Yes! And not by choice!

DAD   Now, Susie, I don't think Charlie played his music loudly knowing it would disturb everyone. It was an accident.

GRANDPA   Bothering others is easy to do if we're not careful. I have started cutting our grass later in the morning because Mrs. Miles, our nice next-door neighbor, likes to sleep late, and I was waking her up with the lawn mower.

CHARLIE   That was very nice of you, Grandpa. I guess I need to be more conscious about being courteous and thoughtful.

GRANDPA   Yes, Charlie, maybe you could memorize Romans 12:18 with me.

CHARLIE   What does Romans 12:18 say, Grandpa?

GRANDPA   Romans 12:18 says, "If possible, so far as it depends on you, be at peace with all men" (NASB). Believe me, it's a lot more peaceful when we try to be courteous and think of others.

CHARLIE   I see your point. I surely seemed to get everyone mad at me today.

GRANDMA   *(Loudly)* Charlie! Would you speak up? I can't hear you. Some loud noise broke my hearing aid!

DAD   Charlie was just going to go get your extra hearing aid, right, Charlie?

CHARLIE   I'm history!

Like Two Peas in a Pod

Characters

Girl puppet
Boy puppet
Grandma puppet

Props

A few frozen peas or small green puffballs.

(Peas are flying in the air, with no puppets onstage yet.)

SUSIE   *(From backstage)* Charlie, quit throwing your peas at me!

CHARLIE   *(From backstage)* Who's going to stop me? Dad and Mom are gone.

SUSIE   Then take that! *(Peas fly through the air.)*

CHARLIE   Susie, you just got peas in my milk.

(Peas go in both directions now. Laughing, etc.)

SUSIE   *(Still backstage)* Charlie, you just hit me on the head.

CHARLIE   *(Still backstage)* That's what they must call a pea brain!

(ALL three puppets come up. CHARLIE and SUSIE have peas taped all over their noses, hair, etc.)

GRANDMA   Charlie and Susie, look at this mess. What are your parents going to say when they get home? They won't be able to trust me to baby-sit again!

SUSIE   I'm sorry, Grandma. We got kind of carried away.

CHARLIE   I don't like peas to eat, Grandma. I only like them for my pea shooter.

GRANDMA   Peas are good for you, Charlie. They help people grow strong, healthy bodies. God expects people to take care of the bodies he made for them by eating right.

SUSIE   Grandma, how do you know so much about what God wants people to do? You are so wise.

GRANDMA   Thank you, Susie. The closer a person gets with God, the more she knows what he expects her to do.

CHARLIE   How does a person get closer with God?

GRANDMA   James 4:8 says, "Draw near to God and He will draw near to you" (NASB).

SUSIE   Well, how does a person draw near to God?

GRANDMA   By reading the Bible and praying. And confessing your sin to God.

CHARLIE   But Grandma, do you have any other secrets?

GRANDMA   One secret, Charlie.

CHARLIE and SUSIE   What, Grandma? Tell us.

SUSIE   I love secrets.

GRANDMA   A good thing for a person who wants to follow God closely is to ask in each different situation, "What would Jesus do or say in this situation?" and then do it.

SUSIE   I'm going to remember that, Grandma! "What would Jesus do or say?"

GRANDMA   Now we need to get this mess cleaned up before your parents get home. (Looks down)

SUSIE   We surely made a mess.

CHARLIE   You know, Grandma, how you are always telling Susie and me we are like two peas in a pod?

GRANDMA   Yes.

CHARLIE   Well, a person should be like two peas in a pod with Jesus.

GRANDMA   That's a good way to remember how a person should act and talk.

CHARLIE   Let's get this mess cleaned up.

SUSIE   Okay. I need to get on my homework.

CHARLIE   This pea wants to split and go outside and play. Get it? Split pea!

GRANDMA   Charlie, you keep telling jokes like that and you'll end up in the soup.

SUSIE   I get it: split pea soup! You're not only wise, Grandma, you're funny. I like it when you baby-sit us.

CHARLIE   Me, too.

You Snooze, You Lose

Characters

Boy puppet
Girl puppet
Mom puppet
Dog puppet (optional)

Props

An alarm clock; child-size cleaning utensils such as mini broom or a dust cloth; signs that say "Next Morning" and "Five Hours Later"

(Alarm clock rings and rings; then put it under a blanket or towel. Make noise of trying to hit it. Finally it stops. CHARLIE comes up, hair all disheveled, pajamas a mess.)

CHARLIE   *(Very slowly)* Is it morning? My clock must be wrong. *(Lays head sideways and sleeps, snoring, etc.)*

MOM   *(From offstage)* Charlie! Charlie, are you up?

CHARLIE   Huh? What? *(Shakes head)* Sure, Mom. *(Goes back to sleep)*

MOM   *(Wait a couple of seconds and come up)* Charlie, get up; you are going to be late for school. I made your favorite breakfast, waffles. *(MOM shakes CHARLIE.)*

CHARLIE   Okay, Mom. *(CHARLIE gets up.)*

MOM   Hurry, son, so you will have time to eat your waffles. *(MOM leaves.)*

CHARLIE   *(Grunts with eyes closed. He falls back offstage, out of sight, and all you hear is snoring. After a couple of seconds his head comes up.)* What's that smell? MMMMM, waffles. I had better hurry. My favorite. *(Goes down; clothes fly up, etc.)*

(MOM and CHARLIE come up.)

MOM   Good morning, son.

CHARLIE   I'm starving; I can't wait to dig into your yummy waffles.

MOM   Here comes the bus! You won't have time for breakfast, Charlie. Bye, kids. Do a good job today.

CHARLIE   How am I supposed to do a good job on an empty stomach?

SUSIE   Hurry! We'll miss the bus!

(EVERYONE leaves. Bring up sign: Next Morning. Optional: Let DOG walk across with sign.)

(Alarm sounds. CHARLIE comes up disheveled as before.)

CHARLIE   Dumb alarm clock. Don't you know it's Saturday? I don't have to get up. *(Snores)*

(DOG with sign: Five Hours Later)

CHARLIE   *(Comes up)* Where is everybody?

MOM   Charlie, are you just getting up?

CHARLIE   Yes, where is everybody? It's lunchtime.

MOM   We all got up and did our chores this morning. We're leaving now to stop and get some chicken and have a picnic. There's a new Christian music group playing in the park which Susie wants to hear.

CHARLIE   The Raptures! Oh, I want to go!

MOM   You have to do your chores now, Charlie. Grandma is in the backyard. You can walk down with her when you're done.

CHARLIE   I'll hurry. *(Dust cloth, broom, mop, etc. come in air.)* Finally, I'm done!

SUSIE   *(Comes up)* Hi, Charlie! You should have heard the Raptures. They were super!

CHARLIE   Is the concert over already?

SUSIE   Yes.

CHARLIE   I missed it!

MOM   Charlie, you sure are missing a lot because you're not getting up in the mornings.

CHARLIE   I know. Waffles yesterday and the Raptures today!

MOM   Charlie, the Bible warns us in Proverbs about sleeping too much. Listen to this verse from Proverbs 6:9, "But you—all you do is sleep. When will you wake up?" (TLB).

CHARLIE   Those verses sound like me. I'm going to try to do better. Mom, will you help me?

MOM   I surely will, Charlie, if you're willing to try.

SUSIE   Can I help? Can I help? My counselor at camp used to get cold water and throw it on the girls who wouldn't get up.

CHARLIE   No thanks, Susie. I'd rather have Mom's help.

MOM   Cold water . . . sounds like a good idea.

CHARLIE   Mommmmm!

MOM   It won't matter anyway, Charlie. You will be getting up on time. I will help you get to bed earlier.

CHARLIE   Right, Mom. I just thought of a way to remember the verses you read in Proverbs.

MOM   How's that?

CHARLIE   You snooze, you lose!

MOM   I like that, Charlie!

Words That Hurt; Words That Help

Characters

Girl puppet
Boy puppet
Mom puppet

SUSIE   Charlie, you are wrrrroooonnnggg!

CHARLIE   Me! Wrong? Can't be!

SUSIE   Listen here, Scuz-Bucket. I said you were wrong!

CHARLIE   You must have your ponytails too tight!

SUSIE   Put a cork in it, Charlie.

CHARLIE   Listen here you hockey puck, I'm not wrong!

SUSIE   All right, Buzzard-Breath, I said you were wrong, and you're wrong!

MOM   Charlie Donald Green and Susie Marie Green, lower your voices. Where in the world did you learn all those words?

CHARLIE   That's how the brothers and sister talk to each other on the new family T.V. show we watched last night.

SUSIE   Yes, Mom, they're always putting each other down. It's funny and cute, especially the littlest brother.

MOM   It is not funny and cute in this house.

CHARLIE   But Mom, if brothers and sisters cut each other down on T.V., why can't Susie and I?

MOM   Charlie, since when are we learning what is right or wrong from the T.V.? I cannot think of a worse example for you to follow.

SUSIE   Whose example should we follow?

MOM   The Book of Ephesians has two very good verses about the words we speak. Listen to one of them. "Let no unwholesome word proceed from your mouth, but only such a word as is good for edification according to the need of the moment, that it may give grace to those who hear (Eph. 4:29 NASB)."

SUSIE   The words we were saying were not very wholesome.

CHARLIE   What does *edification* mean, Mom?

MOM   It means helping another person by the words you say.

CHARLIE   Uh oh, we weren't doing that at all.

SUSIE   What's the other verse, Mom?

MOM   It's in the next chapter, Ephesians 5:4: "And there must be no filthiness and silly talk, or coarse jesting, which are not fitting, but rather giving of thanks" (NASB).

SUSIE   Boy, our words sounded like all those bad things the Bible says we shouldn't say.

CHARLIE   I'm sorry, Susie.

SUSIE   Me too, Charlie.

MOM   Good, kids. Now I want you both to run upstairs, get your Bibles, look up both of these verses, and read them. Then I want you to memorize one of them before supper. *(MOM leaves.)*

CHARLIE and SUSIE   Okay, Mom.

SUSIE   Which one of the verses are you going to memorize, Charlie?

CHARLIE   I don't know yet. I've got to go count the words in each verse and see which one is shorter.

Honesty is the Best Policy

Characters

Girl puppet
Boy puppet
Dad puppet
Mom puppet
Grandma puppet

Prop

Tape of phone ringing, then of doorbell sound

(ALL puppets, except GRANDMA, come up.)

DAD   Isn't this nice, to be able to relax after church and such a good Sunday dinner?

CHARLIE, SUSIE, and MOM   Surely is, Dad.

SUSIE   That meatloaf was good, Mom.

MOM   Thank you, Susie. The dishes went fast with all four of us working together.

DAD   This is just a perfect, relaxing day. I think I'll take a *(PHONE rings.)* nice nap. *(PHONE rings again.)*

CHARLIE   I'll get it. *(CHARLIE disappears.)*

MOM   You deserve a nap, dear. You've been working so hard all week.

CHARLIE   *(Comes back up)* Dad, the phone's for you.

DAD   Who is it?

CHARLIE   Sounds like work.

DAD   Charlie, run and tell them I'm out and you don't know when I'll be back. I do not want to go to work.

CHARLIE   Well, okay Dad. Are you sure that's right?

DAD   It's fine, son. I've been working all week. They can call someone else.

(CHARLIE disappears.)

MOM   I think I'll read the paper. *(CHARLIE comes back up.)* Now, where is the paper?

(DOORBELL rings.)

SUSIE   I'll get it this time.

(SUSIE disappears.)

MOM   Did Caleb run off with that paper again?

SUSIE   *(Comes back)* Mom, it's Bertha here to see you.

MOM   Oh, no! Susie, go tell her I'm taking a nap.

SUSIE   Well, okay, Mom. If you say so. *(SUSIE leaves.)*

MOM   Now, where's that paper? *(MOM leaves.)*

DAD   I'll help you find it, and then I'm off to take my nap. (DAD leaves.)

(SUSIE comes back and joins CHARLIE.)

SUSIE   Charlie, could you call Pam for me and tell her I'm sick, so she won't come over. She's supposed to come and help me with math. My teacher told her to, and she's been bugging me about coming. I don't want to study today.

CHARLIE   Well, okay, but first I think I'll have another piece of pie.

SUSIE   Mom said we could only have one. The last piece is for Dad.

CHARLIE   Well, if Dad asks me, I'll tell him Mom ate it, and if Mom asks me, I'll tell her Dad ate it.

SUSIE   Sounds pretty smart to me.

(BOTH disappear.)

DAD   (Appears) Come on, kids, time for night church. Hurry up, dear, we'll be late.

(ALL FOUR come up and they go off together.)

(DAD starts at far right of stage, comes in with head down, stays sideways, and goes across to left of stage. MOM follows exact same way, about a foot behind. Then CHARLIE and then SUSIE. Each stays sideways, like a prison lineup.)

(GRANDMA comes up on left.)

GRANDMA   Why do you all look so dejected? You look like a prison lineup.

(ENTIRE FAMILY turn together and face audience. To get this turn together, have the DAD puppeteer hold up 1-2-3 fingers and turn on three.)

DAD   We just came from church.

GRANDMA   I know. I wish I had felt good enough to go with you. I'm feeling a little better now, though.

MOM   We're not.

GRANDMA   What did Pastor [Skorheim] (insert your pastor's name here if performing for a church) speak on tonight?

CHARLIE   Proverbs 3:3: "Do not let kindness and truth leave you; bind them around your neck, write them on the tablet of your heart" (NASB).

GRANDMA   That sounds like a wonderful verse. It is so easy to get caught up in lying. The old saying from when I was little girl doesn't seem to apply anymore.

SUSIE   What saying, Grandma?

GRANDMA   "Honesty is always the best policy." It seems men lie to their bosses so much today: "I'm sick." Or they have someone lie on the phone. (DAD hangs head.) It's such a shame. I've seen mothers have their children lie for them. It is so sad, because they teach their children to lie instead of to be honest. Actions speak more loudly than words. (MOM hangs head.) Then children lie because they see their parents lie, and then no one pleases God with an honest heart. (CHARLIE and SUSIE hang heads.)

DAD   Children, we need to have a family meeting.

GRANDMA   I'll leave. I'm still feeling weak. (GRANDMA leaves.)

DAD   All of us have been dishonest. Your Mom and I have been wrong.

MOM   We've made a mistake.

CHARLIE   Dad and Mom, so have I. I ate the last piece of pie.

SUSIE   I lied to Pam.

80

DAD   Let's all start trying to be more honest.

MOM   We can all help each other.

SUSIE   I like God's promise which Pastor [Skorheim] told us follows the verse about not lying. Proverbs 3:4 says, "You will find favor and good repute in the sight of God and man" (NASB).

DAD   I'm sure I lost favor at work because of my lie.

MOM   We've learned a valuable lesson today.

(PHONE rings.)

CHARLIE   I'll get it. Is everybody really home?

MOM, DAD, and SUSIE   Charlieeeee!

CHARLIE   Just kidding! It feels good to be honest! You don't have to remember what you say!

I Dare You

Characters

Boy puppet
Girl puppet
Mom puppet

Props

Bandages and black felt for bruises for
Charlie

(SUSIE and MOM appear.)

SUSIE   Boy, Mom, what a great day today!

CHARLIE   *(From backstage groaning)*
OHHH . . . aaugh . . . ouuuch . . .

MOM   *(Looking at SUSIE)* My, what is that
terrible noise?

SUSIE   I don't know. It sounds like a cow
who isn't feeling too well.

CHARLIE   *(From backstage and louder)*
Ohhhh . . . aaugh . . . ouuuch . . .

MOM   That sounds a little like your
brother!

SUSIE   I think you're right.

*(CHARLIE appears with bandages placed all
over his head and body.)*

CHARLIE   *(Hanging head low)* I've never
hurt so much in my life!

MOM   Charlie, are you hurt? What
happened?

CHARLIE   Well, I think I'll say what
Grandma always says: "What don't
hurt, don't work!" Ohhh . . .

MOM   Charlie, how did you get so
banged up?

CHARLIE   Do you know that steep wind-
ing trail behind the school in the
woods?

MOM   Yes.

CHARLIE   I rode my bike down it today.

SUSIE   Charlie, are you crazy? That's not
even safe to walk down, no less ride
your bike down. Why in the world
did you do that?

CHARLIE   Well, Larry and his gang told
me no one had ever made it all the
way down that hill. They dared me
and then bet I couldn't do it, either.
You know, they were right, I didn't
make it! Ohhh . . . .

MOM   Who bandaged you?

CHARLIE   The school nurse.

MOM   Charlie, you mean to say you rode
down that hill just on a dare?

CHARLIE   Oh, no, Mom! It wasn't just a
dare. It was a triple kings X dare. You
know, the worst kind.

MOM   Charlie, you mean you crashed your bike in the bushes and risked being really hurt just for a dare?

CHARLIE   Well, it wasn't the bushes; it was a pine tree. I was kind of up close and personal with that tree. I feel like a real sap!

SUSIE   What would Larry and his gang have said if you hadn't taken that dare?

CHARLIE   They would have called me a sissy.

SUSIE   Big deal! Tomorrow at school they'll be calling you stupid!

MOM   Charlie, what would they have said if you had made it all the way down the hill?

CHARLIE   Hm-m, come to think of it, they would have just called me "lucky" and rode off on their bikes.

MOM   I have a verse in the Bible for you, Charlie. Your grandma had me learn this when I was a kid. Proverbs 1:10: "My son, if sinners entice thee, consent thou not" (KJV).

SUSIE   Mom, what does *entice* mean?

MOM   It's when someone tries to get you to do something you don't want to do or something you know you shouldn't do.

CHARLIE   That makes sense. I didn't want to ride down that trail, and I knew I shouldn't, but I did.

SUSIE   In other words, we shouldn't accept dares.

MOM   Yes, Susie, sometimes you just have to say no even if you know you will get called names. Kids who dare you really aren't your friends, anyway. A true friend would not want you to risk getting hurt or in trouble.

CHARLIE   I see your point.

MOM   I think you both have learned something. Now I want you two to get started on your homework.

SUSIE   Charlie, I dare you to do my homework.

MOM   Susie!

SUSIE   Sorry, Mom, I wouldn't dare to have Charlie do my homework!

CHARLIE   Don't worry, Mom, I'm not falling for dares anymore anyway.

MOM   Good boy, Charlie.

Jesus, Others, You

Characters

Boy puppet
Girl puppet
Mom puppet
Grandma puppet

Props

You might make a poster to hang on the outside of the stage or cover:

Jesus
Others
You

From it the audience can better visualize what this sketch is teaching. Another idea would be to make a bookmark for each child with this on it. This is an important scriptural truth for today. Our society is "rights" demanding, and kids are constantly being told to look out for number one. The extra work to send something home from the puppets could serve as a small reminder of this scriptural truth.

(Door slam; optional)

CHARLIE   Mom! We're home!

SUSIE   Mom! Where are you? We've got some great news.

MOM   *(MOM and GRANDMA come up.)* Hi kids! Sorry I didn't hear you come in. Grandma and I were in the kitchen making some cookies for the people in the rest home down the street. The church is sending a group this Saturday.

GRANDMA   What's this about great news, Susie?

SUSIE   I got a math award today at school during the awards assembly.

CHARLIE   I got the spelling award.

MOM   How great, Charlie and Susie! As usual, I'm proud of you.

GRANDMA   Sounds like Susie got her grandpa's head for numbers and Charlie his grandma's ability to spell.

MOM   Did anyone else we know get an award at the assembly?

CHARLIE   John White got the good-citizen award for helping Mrs. Andrews with chores around her house. She has trouble doing some things now, since she fell and hurt her hip and leg.

MOM   That's really great.

SUSIE   What's so great? He did it for free! That just doesn't add up to much when counting your money in your piggy bank.

GRANDMA   Susie, it doesn't add up here on earth, but it surely does in heaven!

MOM   It's nice John did get an award, but the main thing is he was thoughtful and willing to help others just for the joy of helping.

GRANDMA   That joy is something money can't buy.

CHARLIE   Yes, he said it made him feel really good inside to know that what he was doing helped someone else.

MOM   There is joy when we help others.

GRANDMA   That's right, kids, but there is something even more important than the joy we have when we help others.

SUSIE   Really? What is that, Grandma?

GRANDMA   We are obeying God when we help others. God has told us in the Bible, in Philippians 2:3–4, that we are to think about others before we think about ourselves.

SUSIE   I learned Philippians 2:4 at camp last year.

CHARLIE   Wow! I just learned the verse before it, Philippians 2:3, in Sunday school.

MOM   Why don't you say them for us? Charlie, you first.

CHARLIE   Philippians 2:3: "Do nothing from selfishness or empty conceit, but with humility of mind let each of you regard one another as more important than himself" (NASB).

SUSIE   Philippians 2:4: "Do not merely look out for your own personal interests but also for the interests of others" (NASB).

MOM   These verses show us how to have true JOY.

GRANDMA   I've always heard Joy—J-O-Y—described as the J of joy for Jesus, O of joy for others, Y for you. When you keep them in the right order, what do they spell?

CHARLIE   J

SUSIE   O

CHARLIE   Y—JOY!

MOM   That's my good speller!

SUSIE   Charlie, let's do what God says and help others.

CHARLIE   Okay, then we'll have real J-O-Y—Jesus, Others, You—Joy!

SUSIE   It surely "adds" up our rewards in heaven!

CHARLIE   What could we do to help someone?

GRANDMA   You could "help" me by tasting the cookies we made for the people in the rest home for Saturday's visit.

SUSIE and CHARLIE   Yes! Sounds great!

SUSIE   And then Mrs. Baker needs her garden weeded. She hasn't felt well all week.

CHARLIE   We could help Grandma and Mom clean up the kitchen.

SUSIE   Wow, there is a lot we can do when we start looking out for others' interests as Jesus told people to do.

CHARLIE   We'll just have to keep our eyes open looking for ways to help others. Helping others is so much better than being selfish!

MOM   I'm going to help you by bringing you a glass of Kool-Aid while you work.

GRANDMA   A drink for my "Kool" grandkids while they "Aid" others.

CHARLIE and SUSIE   (Groan) Grandma, then we'll help you find a new joke book!

Pride Goes Before a Fall

Characters

Dad puppet
Boy puppet
Girl puppet

Props

Pair of sunglasses for Susie

(DAD comes up looking down and thoughtful.)

CHARLIE   (Comes up and looks at Dad) Dad, what are you thinking about?

DAD   I was thinking about my Sunday school lesson for tomorrow. I need a way to help the boys and girls in my class understand the story of John the Baptist.

CHARLIE   Oh! I like John the Baptist. He was Jesus' cousin.

DAD   Right, son.

CHARLIE   I didn't like what he ate though: locusts. Eating grasshoppers, yuck!

DAD   That would "bug" me too, son.

CHARLIE   Very funny, Dad! I know what you could do for your class.

DAD   What?

CHARLIE   You could have two of the kids act out a scene between Jesus and John the Baptist.

DAD   That's a good idea, Charlie.

(SUSIE enters with sunglasses.)

SUSIE   Did I hear someone say act?

DAD   Susie, how would you and Charlie like to act out a play between John the Baptist and Jesus for me so I could see how it would work with my Sunday school class?

SUSIE   Sure, Dad. I'd love to act for you. I always knew I'd be a star someday! (Throws hair back)

CHARLIE   That's perfect, you being a star. You belong in outer space.

DAD   Okay, kids, be nice or we won't be able to practice this play.

CHARLIE   Alright.

SUSIE   What's the play about?

DAD   About John the Baptist's humility.

SUSIE and CHARLIE   What's humility?

DAD   Why don't you look it up in a dictionary, Charlie?

CHARLIE   Okay. (Sound of paper behind screen: just wrinkle your script.) *Humility*—"lack of pride."

CHARLIE and SUSIE   (Together) Dad, what's pride?

DAD   (Laughing) Pride is when you think too much of yourself or your ability.

SUSIE   You mean we're not to have confidence in things we can do well?

DAD   No, that is not what I mean, Susie. Romans 12:3 says, "I say to every man among you not to think more highly of himself than he ought to think; but to think so as to have sound judgment" (NASB). That means we are to have an accurate or right view of ourselves. God has given all of us talents and abilities. We need to realize he gives us ability to do some things well.

SUSIE   You mean like God giving me the ability to act?

DAD   Right, Susie. You did a good job in the Easter play at church. God has given you an ability to act. You need to thank him for your ability and not take all the credit yourself. We have confidence, but it is in God and the ability he gives us.

SUSIE   If all our talents and abilities come from God, we can't brag about them.

DAD   That's right. If we brag about ourselves or put other people down who do not have the same ability, that would be pride.

CHARLIE   Well, Dad, what do you want Susie and me to do in the play practice for your Sunday school class?

DAD   (Whispers plans offstage to first CHARLIE, then SUSIE.)

SUSIE   This is going to be fun. I'm going to get ready! Makeup!

CHARLIE   A star is born!

Choosing Sides

Characters

Boy puppet
Girl puppet
Dad puppet
Mom puppet

(CHARLIE and SUSIE both appear.)

(Optional: CHARLIE, or both CHARLIE and SUSIE, wearing baseball hats)

SUSIE   I'm so embarrassed, Charlie Green. How could you do this to me?

CHARLIE   Well, it's true, you are a klutz, and you can't play ball!

SUSIE   Well, maybe I'm not the greatest softball player, but you didn't have to announce it to the whole neighborhood!

(DAD and MOM appear.)

DAD   My goodness, you two, we heard you from way upstairs.

MOM   What in the world is the matter?

SUSIE   Charlie embarrassed me in front of the whole neighborhood. I'll never be able to show my face outside this house again!

CHARLIE   Susie's exaggerating. It wasn't the whole neighborhood. Harold is visiting his aunt, and he wasn't there.

SUSIE   Oh, big whoopie! It was only in front of eighteen kids, not nineteen!

CHARLIE   *(Meekly)* Well, it wasn't the whole neighborhood.

MOM   Susie, what did Charlie do?

SUSIE   We were choosing sides for softball, and Charlie told everybody I was so uncoordinated I couldn't walk and chew gum at the same time.

MOM   Charlie, that wasn't very nice.

SUSIE   Then he said I threw so bad that for someone to say I threw like a girl would be a compliment and he'd never pick me for his team.

DAD   Charlie, sometimes it's more important to make others feel good about themselves than to just pick the kids you think will help you win the game. The Bible says very little about winning games, but God's Word says a lot about how we treat others.

MOM   Your dad is right. Remember when he was given those tickets to the ball game, but instead he went to Aunt Helen's birthday party?

CHARLIE   Yes, I know Dad really wanted to go to that ball game, too.

MOM   Yes, he did, but your dad wanted to honor Aunt Helen rather than have a good time himself.

DAD   Yes, Charlie, I did want to see that game, but remember what we just learned in church. Romans 12:10: "Be devoted to one another in brotherly love. Give preference to one another in honor" (NASB).

CHARLIE   So you mean we should do things for others to make them feel good, even if it costs us something?

MOM   When we love and honor someone, we put them above ourselves and want their best rather than ours.

CHARLIE   I see. So I should have picked Susie to be on my team over some of the better players who wouldn't care if they were picked last.

DAD   You're getting the idea now! I remember when I was in the eleventh grade I was picked next to last every time we played basketball.

SUSIE   Dad, you mean basketball was invented already when you were a boy?

DAD   (Laughing) Yes, Susie! I still remember the hurt of not being chosen or wanted.

CHARLIE   That's sad. Dad, maybe we shouldn't even be choosing teams.

MOM   I think that would be the best, Charlie. Instead of choosing teams, why not have an adult who would be fair appoint the teams?

SUSIE   If an adult isn't around, we could draw numbers.

DAD   Those are great ideas. Sometimes, though, you kids will be involved in picking teams where you can't get out of it. Like me when I was in school. For those times remember the verse in Romans 12:10 to treat others with love and honor.

CHARLIE   (Turning to Susie) Susie, next time we play softball I'm going to choose you first.

SUSIE   Thanks, Charlie!

CHARLIE   Yep, old Slugger Susie.

SUSIE   Let's not get carried away. Just not being picked last will be enough. Thanks, Charlie.

Once Jesus' Child, Always His Child

Characters

Boy puppet
Girl puppet
Mom puppet
Dad puppet
Dog puppet

Props

Line of masking tape down center of Dad's face with black and blue on it.

DAD *(Comes up with masking tape line down face)* Charlie Donald Green! Come here.

CHARLIE *(Appears on side of set or out of Dad's sight)* Uh, oh! I must be in trouble. Dad used my middle name, and listen to him.

(Susie and Mom come up.)

MOM What's wrong, dear?

DAD That son of *yours* left the rake in the yard, and I stepped on it, and thump! *(Throw head back for emphasis.)* Now I have this crease down my face.

SUSIE Charlie's in trouble. Here, Dad, let me help you find *Mom's* son.

(SUSIE goes down and comes up with CHARLIE.)

SUSIE Here's the culprit, Dad. You don't have to put out an APB to find him. By the way, is there a reward?

MOM Susie, this is not the time to tease Dad.

SUSIE Who's teasing! *(SUSIE leaves.)*

DAD Charlie Donald, did you leave the rake in the yard when you were raking the leaves this morning?

CHARLIE Oops. I was in a hurry to come in for lunch. I forgot to put it away. I was going to finish tomorrow.

DAD What have I told you about putting things away?

CHARLIE I'm sorry, Dad, I was careless. Will you forgive me?

DAD Yes, son.

CHARLIE I heard you call me *Mom's* son. Does this mean I'm only Mom's son and not yours anymore because I left the rake in the yard and you stepped on it?

DAD *(Looking down)* I'm sorry for calling you your mother's son. You will always be my son, too. Sometimes pain and disappointment cause me to say things I don't mean.

CHARLIE I guess we both were wrong and learned our lessons.

DAD   Neither of us are perfect, are we?

MOM   This reminds me of a verse I was reading this morning in Philippians 1:6: "For I am confident of this very thing, that He who began a good work in you will perfect it until the day of Christ Jesus" (NASB).

CHARLIE   You mean God is always working on people who believe in him?

DAD   You're right, son. He begins working when people accept Jesus into their hearts and keeps helping or perfecting them until they go to heaven.

CHARLIE   What happens if people sin? Do they stop being God's child?

MOM   No. Once people have Jesus in their hearts he never leaves. He is always with them helping them to grow. If they do something, they need only to ask Jesus to forgive them just like you and Dad asked each other to forgive.

DAD   One of my favorite verses is John 10:28. Jesus is speaking and says, "I give eternal life to them, and they shall never perish; and no one shall snatch them out of my hand" (NASB).

CHARLIE   Once a person is Jesus' child, no matter what, he is always Jesus' child. I wish John White could hear this. He has raised his hand every Sunday when the teacher has asked the boys and girls if they want to ask Jesus into their hearts.

DAD   Some people think when they do something wrong that they are no longer Jesus' child and they need to ask Jesus into their hearts again. But these verses show people who accept Jesus that they are *always* Jesus' children. Once Jesus is in a person's heart, he never leaves.

MOM   Charlie, asking Jesus over and over to come into a person's heart when he is already in the heart would be like me asking you to come into this room right now.

CHARLIE   That's silly, Mom! I'm already in this room.

MOM   You're right. It's the same way once Jesus is in your heart. You don't need to keep asking him.

SUSIE   *(Susie enters with Caleb.)* Caleb just chewed on Charlie's baseball mitt.

CHARLIE   Caleb! You're a bad dog.

(Caleb hangs his head.)

CHARLIE   I forgive you. I still love you, Caleb, and you're still my dog.

(Caleb barks and rubs up against Charlie.)

DAD   That's *my* son!

Helping the Aging Gracefully

Characters

Dad puppet
Mom puppet
Boy puppet
Girl puppet
Grandma puppet

(*DAD and CHARLIE come up.*)

DAD   Anybody home? Charlie and I are back from the hardware store.

(*MOM and SUSIE come up.*)

MOM   Hi! It seemed to take you all a long time. Did you buy the store out?

CHARLIE   (*Aggravated and disgusted*) No, we got behind this *old (Say slowly and dramatically)* geezer coming home; and he was driving so slowly *(Say slowly and dramatically)*; and we couldn't pass him. It took F-O-R-E-V-E-R *(Say slowly and drawn out)* to get home, and now I've missed the baseball game in the park.

SUSIE   I know what you mean, Charlie. Old people drive and walk soooo s-l-o-w-l-y *(Say slowly and drawn out)*. It's a wonder they get anyplace!

CHARLIE   Yes, I think watching old people walk is what gave someone the idea for s-l-o-w m-o-t-i-o-n *(Say slowly and drawn out)* on T.V. replays.

DAD   Charlie and Susie, I'm very disappointed to hear you both talking this way about people God made and loves.

MOM   God has everyone on earth for a purpose, no matter what their age.

DAD   Charlie, do you remember when you had your leg in a cast last summer?

CHARLIE   Yes, that was awful. I was so frustrated because I couldn't get around and do things. I didn't like it.

DAD   Charlie, that's how older people feel.

MOM   They would like to be able to move faster and do things more quickly like they could when they were young, but they can't. Their bodies won't let them.

DAD   They are frustrated sometimes just like you were, Charlie, when you had your leg in a cast.

SUSIE   Oh! That would be hard not to be able to do things you would like to do.

DAD   The Bible tells us in 1 Timothy 5:1–2 that we need to treat older men and older women as we would our fathers and mothers.

MOM   Remember when we were memorizing the Ten Commandments? The

Bible says to honor our father and mother.

DAD   We are to honor all older people; in other words, treat them with respect.

CHARLIE   It doesn't please God when people make fun of older people or call them names like old geezer, does it?

MOM   No, Charlie, it doesn't. It's not right ever. Some people will be nice to older people and hold the door for them, but when they get into a car to drive they act differently and are rude. No matter where or when we see an older person having a difficult time, we should be patient and respectful.

SUSIE   Charlie and I were wrong. From now on I'm going to be nice and helpful to older people.

CHARLIE   Me, too, because that would please God.

GRANDMA   *(Comes up)* Hi, you all. I decided to walk over for a visit. How is everyone?

CHARLIE and SUSIE   Hi, Grandma!

SUSIE   You must be tired and thirsty from your walk. Here, let me get you something to drink.

CHARLIE   Why don't you go over and sit in the big soft chair in the living room.

GRANDMA   How nice of you kids. I haven't forgotten a birthday or something, have I?

MOM   No, we were just talking about how God wants us to treat older people with respect and love.

SUSIE   It's easy to show Grandma we love her. She's special.

GRANDMA   Thanks, Susie!

CHARLIE   That man if front of us today could have been someone's grandpa.

DAD   That's right, Charlie. We need to treat all our older friends like we would want others to treat our special grandma.

SUSIE   Grandma, when you get ready to walk home, I'll walk with you.

CHARLIE   Me, too, Grandma.

GRANDMA   Are you sure, kids? I walk kind of slowly. *(Say slowly and drawn out.)*

CHARLIE   We don't mind, Grandma. You can see more that way!

Vandalism: It's Not Entertainment

Characters

Dad puppet
Mom puppet
Boy puppet
Girl puppet

(DAD alone comes up.)

DAD   *(Slowly and loudly)* Chaaarrrlie! Chaaarrrlie!

CHARLIE   Hi, Dad! What's up?

DAD   Charlie, I had a very disturbing call from Mrs. Johnson down the street.

CHARLIE   *(Meekly)* Oh, Mrs. Johnson.

(SUSIE and MOM appear.)

SUSIE   Hi, Charlie! Mom and I saw you and some other guys coming out of the hardware store. It looks like you were buying spray paint.

MOM   Yes, Charlie, are you finally going to paint your bike?

(CHARLIE looks at audience.)

CHARLIE   Oh boy! I am in trouble!

DAD   Charlie! So it was you!

MOM   What are you talking about, dear?

DAD   Mrs. Johnson called and said she saw some boys running from her back fence, and someone had painted

"C. G. was here" with blue spray paint!

(MOM looking at CHARLIE)

MOM   That C.G. wouldn't stand for Charlie Green, would it?

SUSIE   You wouldn't do that, would you Charlie?

CHARLIE   You had to ask?

SUSIE   But, Charlie, you like Mrs. Johnson. Why would you wreck her fence?

CHARLIE   I didn't want to wreck it. We were just bored and wanted to do something entertaining.

MOM   Charlie, when we break or vandalize other people's property, that goes beyond fun.

CHARLIE   What's vandalism?

MOM   Vandalism is when you don't necessarily break something, but you scratch it, or bend it, or . . .

CHARLIE   Or paint on it.

MOM   Yes, painting on someone's fence is vandalism.

DAD   Anytime someone paints on a fence, or breaks a window out of an abandoned building, or does something bad to someone else's property, that is vandalism.

MOM   You know, Charlie, in our Bible study at church we learned from the Book of Genesis that we were placed on earth to take care of it. Listen to Genesis 2:15: "Then the LORD God took the man and put him into the Garden of Eden to cultivate it and keep it" (NASB).

DAD   Just as God placed Adam and Eve to be in charge of the garden of Eden, so we need to care for our world, and that starts with our neighborhood.

CHARLIE   I see. God wants us to take care of our neighborhood, and vandalism surely doesn't show I'm taking care of our neighborhood.

MOM   Charlie, I think you're getting the point.

CHARLIE   I need to go back to the store to buy some more paint.

DAD, MOM, and SUSIE   More paint!

CHARLIE   Yes, I need to go and paint Mrs. Johnson's fence back to the color it was.

DAD   That's a way to make up for it. But, remember, anytime you destroy something, that's not fun—it's vandalism, and God doesn't want us to vandalize.

CHARLIE   Yes, Dad, I understand now.

SUSIE   Hey, Charlie, I might even help you repaint Mrs. Johnson's fence. Mom, is it vandalism if you paint on someone, say your brother, while you're helping him paint?

CHARLIE   Thanks, anyway, for the offer to help, Susie, but it sounds like this is a one-boy job.

This Little Light of Mine

Characters

Boy puppet
Girl puppet
Mom puppet

Prop

Flashlight

(CHARLIE comes up with hand mover and flashlight taped to his hand; starts shining light in audience's eyes.)

SUSIE   Charlie, what are you doing?

CHARLIE   I'm using my new flashlight to see where I'm going.

SUSIE   *(Sighs)* Charlie, don't you know anything? You don't need a flashlight when it's daytime and light outside. You only need a light when it's dark.

MOM   What are you doing with your flashlight, Charlie?

SUSIE   Mom, Charlie is using his flashlight during the day! Can you believe that? I think he's *light* on brains. *(SUSIE laughs.)* I'm laughing so hard I feel *light* headed. I continually amaze myself. I'm *light*ening fast when it comes to saying something funny.

MOM   Charlie, why are you using your flashlight now during the day?

CHARLIE   This morning in Sunday school our teacher told us the world is dark, and we need to shine our lights. We sang the song "This Little Light of Mine."

SUSIE   I know that song. *(Start singing)* "This little light of mine, I'm going to let it shine . . ."

MOM   Thank you, Susie. I know the song Charlie is talking about.

SUSIE   What was Charlie's teacher talking about when she said the world is dark. I don't get it! It seems light to me.

MOM   Charlie's teacher was saying the world is dark because of the sin in the world. People often use the word *dark* to describe sin. Saying the world is dark with sin is just a picture for our minds to help understand the sin in people's lives who live in the world.

CHARLIE   You mean shining my flashlight won't help light up the dark world?

MOM   No, Charlie. The light your teacher was talking about is not your flashlight but you.

SUSIE   You mean when we sing "This Little Light of Mine" we're talking about us? We're supposed to be lights? It's a good thing I'm a "bright" light. Get it—smart—"bright" light. Ha! Ha! I just continue to amaze myself.

MOM   Yes, we are the lights of the world. Jesus said in Matthew 5:14, "You are the light of the world" (NASB).

CHARLIE   Mom, is light another picture for our minds? I don't understand how I can be a light.

MOM   Two verses later Jesus tell us how we are a light. Listen to Jesus' word and tell me how we are lights. Matthew 5:16: "Let your light shine before men in such a way that they may see your good works, and glorify your Father who is in heaven" (NASB).

CHARLIE   We are lights when we do good works.

MOM   Right. When people are nice to others and live the way the Bible teaches them to live, they are lights for God.

CHARLIE   Oh! I understand. People will want to know why we are lights and do good things and not sin and do bad things. Then we can tell them about God and how he can make them lights by asking Jesus into their hearts to forgive them of their sin.

MOM   Right. When Jesus comes into a person's heart, he takes away the dark sin and makes a person a light.

SUSIE   I haven't been shining my light very brightly by teasing you, Charlie. That's bad. I'm sorry. I want my light to shine brightly so people will want to know about God and his Son Jesus.

MOM   Each person chooses how brightly her light will shine.

SUSIE   Mom, do you remember last night for Dad's birthday how you put those candles on his cake that wouldn't blow out? They kept on burning bright.

CHARLIE   That was so funny! Dad tried and tried to blow them out and couldn't.

MOM   Yes, I remember. Why?

SUSIE   That's how a person should be. She should be a light for Jesus that shines brightly and nothing can blow it out or stop it.

MOM and CHARLIE   Susie, you continually amaze us!

CHARLIE   You are a "bright" light!

Church and Sunday School Are No Fun

Characters

Dad puppet
Mom puppet
Girl puppet
Boy puppet

ALL PUPPETS are sitting in car coming home from Sunday school and church. Arrange them as two adults in front, two children in back.

CHARLIE　*(Hushed tone)* I didn't like church and Sunday school. It wasn't any fun!

SUSIE　You're just mad, Charlie, because you got in trouble in Sunday school this morning. I'm going to tell Dad and Mom.

CHARLIE　You're such a tattletale, Susie!

(Bump into each other when you say your line.)

SUSIE　Am not!

CHARLIE　Are so!

SUSIE　Am not!

CHARLIE　Are so!

SUSIE　Am not a tattletale. I'm not tattling a tale. I'm tattling the truth, so that makes me a tattletruth. So there!

DAD　What are you kids arguing about back there?

SUSIE　Charlie got in trouble in Sunday school this morning. *(Sniffs at Charlie and continues.)* Na-na-na-na.

CHARLIE　*(Under breath)* Tattletale.

DAD　What did you do in Sunday school to get in trouble?

CHARLIE　I was just trying to have some fun.

DAD　What did you do?

CHARLIE　I took the bottom off the world globe bank, and when our teacher picked it up, all the money the kids had put in fell out all over the floor and rolled everywhere. Everyone laughed.

SUSIE　That's not all he did, Dad.

CHARLIE　*(Under breath)* Tattletale.

MOM　What else, son?

CHARLIE　Well, I sorta tied the ties on the back of Laura's dress to her chair. When she got up to go, she took the whole chair with her. Everyone thought it was funny.

SUSIE　That's not all, Dad and Mom.

CHARLIE　*(Under breath)* Tattletale.

MOM　What else, Charlie?

CHARLIE   I hid the teacher's Bible. It was so funny watching her look for it. I was just having fun.

SUSIE   Charlie told me he doesn't think Sunday school is fun.

CHARLIE   *(Under breath)* Tattletale.

MOM   Charlie, the main purpose of Sunday school and church is not to have fun.

DAD   The reason we go to church is to learn about God and what he has told us in the Bible.

MOM   This gives us joy, but we're not in church and Sunday school just for fun. We are there to worship God and to let him know we love him and want to grow closer to him by keeping him first in our week.

CHARLIE   My actions this morning surely didn't let God know I loved him.

MOM   No, son, I think you probably didn't learn anything.

SUSIE   That's right. He was too busy having fun!

DAD   Pastor [Skorheim] *(Insert your pastor's name if in a church)* last week in our Sunday school was telling us parents we should ask our kids what they learned after church or Sunday school and not whether they had fun. He said we should save the question of did they have fun for when we pick you up from a birthday party.

MOM   When we ask what you learned, it helps all of us remember why we are in church and Sunday school.

CHARLIE   To learn! I understand there are times to have fun, but I guess there are times when we need to be serious, too.

DAD   That's a good way to put it, Charlie. When we are listening to the Bible being taught, it is a time to be serious.

SUSIE   Mom and Dad, Charlie was playing tic-tac-toe on the bulletin with Tommy during church.

CHARLIE   *(Under breath)* Tattletale.

MOM   Charlie's not going to do that anymore.

CHARLIE   Right, Mom. I'm going to church and Sunday school to learn about God and the Bible.

DAD   I have an idea. Why don't we start every Sunday on the way home from church and Sunday school telling each other one thing we learned?

SUSIE   That's a good idea.

MOM   You may go first, Susie.

SUSIE   I learned in Sunday school not to be so concerned about other people's faults and sins as you are about your own. You're supposed to keep a lookout for yourself and not tattle on others.

DAD, MOM, and CHARLIE   *(All three laugh.)*

SUSIE   What's everyone laughing about? I don't get it!

DAD   Susie, since we've been in the car you have been tattling on Charlie— just the opposite of what you said you learned.

MOM   When we truly learn lessons from the Bible we don't just listen but we act on them.

SUSIE   *(Laughing)* Oh, that was pretty funny.

CHARLIE   It looks like we all learn when we talk about the things we learned on our way home.

DAD   This will be another good Green family tradition.

Turn the Other Cheek? No Way!

Characters

Boy puppet
Girl puppet
Dad puppet
Mom puppet

Props

Band-Aids

(CHARLIE enters with several Band-Aids on his face.)

CHARLIE *(Looking sad, head drooping)* Ugh, ooooh, ouch!

SUSIE   Charlie Green! What happened to you? You look like you got in a fight with your whole class!

CHARLIE   Not the whole class, just Big Eddie.

SUSIE   Big Eddie! He's so mean, if he smiled his face would crack.

CHARLIE   Yes, I know. Boy, do I know!

SUSIE   What did you do to get him mad at you?

CHARLIE   Well, he called me lizard lips, right in front of all the other guys.

SUSIE   What did you say?

CHARLIE   Well, er, ah, I said, "You're so ugly you have to sneak up on a mirror to comb your hair."

SUSIE   Charlie, that was pretty dumb!

CHARLIE   That's an understatement!

(Enter DAD and MOM)

DAD and MOM   Hi, kids!

MOM   Charlie Green! What happened to you?

CHARLIE   Well, as I just told Susie, I got in a fight with Big Eddie.

DAD   Charlie, was there any way you could have avoided this fight?

CHARLIE   Well, no Dad. He called me lizard lips.

MOM   Charlie, I don't think that's a reason to get in a fight.

CHARLIE   Well, what was I supposed to do? Run away like a chicken?

DAD   You didn't have to run away, but you could have been brave and walked away.

CHARLIE   Brave? How is that being brave?

DAD   Anyone can get into a fight, but it takes a courageous kid to stop a fight, especially if other kids won't understand and maybe call you names. But Jesus said in Matthew 5:9, "Blessed are the peacemakers."

SUSIE   I know what you mean, Dad. Didn't Grandpa Green get a pacemaker last year.

DAD   (Laughing) Susie, not a pacemaker—though that was a blessing to Grandpa—but Jesus said, "Blessed are the *peace*makers." Those are people who don't get into fights.

CHARLIE   You mean, Jesus is happy when we try to make peace instead of fight?

MOM   That's right, Charlie. Here's a verse your grandma had me memorize when I was about your age. Matthew 5:39: "But I say to you, do not resist him who is evil; but whoever slaps you on your right cheek, turn to him the other also" (NASB).

CHARLIE   No way! Turn the other cheek! Does the Bible really say that?

DAD   Yes, it does. Think about it. If you had just ignored Eddie, most likely none of this would have happened.

MOM   When you called him a name back you weren't turning the other cheek, were you?

CHARLIE   No, I guess I wasn't. So what you are saying is if someone starts picking on me or calling me names, I should ignore him or walk away?

DAD   I think you're getting the point.

CHARLIE   I see your point, but that would be hard. It's a lot easier just to get in a fight.

MOM   Charlie, sometimes being a Christian takes a lot of courage and is hard, but it's always worth it.

CHARLIE   You're right, Mom.

SUSIE   So next time we get in a fight you have to turn the other cheek.

CHARLIE   Well, I'm sure sisters don't count.

DAD   Charlie, even sisters count!

CHARLIE   This is going to be harder than I thought. It's a good thing Jesus never asks us to do anything that he doesn't help us do.

MOM   Jesus gave you parents to help sisters learn to turn the other cheek and also not to aggravate their brothers.

SUSIE   I get your point, Mom. You're a real peacemaker!

(CHARLIE and SUSIE leave)

MOM   I'm glad we had this talk with the kids. With all of us working on being peacemakers, we should have some real peace and quiet in our home.

SUSIE   (From offstage) Mom, can Pam White spend the night?

(MOM looks at DAD.)

DAD   There goes our peace and quiet!

Magnify the Lord

Characters

Grandma puppet
Girl puppet

Props

Biggest magnifying glass you can find. Tape hand mover or stick to Susie's hand, along with the magnifying glass, so it looks as if Susie is holding the glass in her hand. Susie needs a *red* hat, cap, or hood on her head.

(*SUSIE comes up walking across stage with GRANDMA behind her. She's looking at ground with magnifying glass.*)

SUSIE   Wow! This is neat. Look at that volcano. I'd better be careful not to fall into it. I'd never get out alive.

GRANDMA   Susie, it's only an ant hole!

(*Next, bring magnifying glass up in front of Susie's eye so audience can see her big eye. Hold glass away and then close for effect. Then have Susie turn to Grandma and hold up the glass. As Susie looks at Grandma through the magnifying glass, she says,*)

SUSIE   (Kind of scared) What big eyes you have, Grandma.

GRANDMA   The better to see you with, my dear.

SUSIE   (*A little more scared*) What big ears you have, Grandma.

GRANDMA   The better to hear you with, my dear.

SUSIE   (*Scared*) What a big mouth you have, Grandma.

GRANDMA   The better to (*pause for effect*) *kiss* my favorite granddaughter.

SUSIE   Phew! I'm glad you said kiss, Grandma, and not, "The better to eat you with, my dear."

GRANDMA   Susie, I think your *red* hat has gone to your head.

SUSIE   Of course, Grandma. Where else would a hat go?

GRANDMA   (*Laugh*) Do you like your new magnifying glass, Susie?

SUSIE   Yes, Grandma, it's such fun to see things bigger. They look so different. But why is it called a magnifying glass?

GRANDMA   Because it magnifies things. In other words, it makes things look bigger.

SUSIE   Magnify means to make things bigger?

GRANDMA   Yes, Susie. It makes things look bigger so you can see what they look like more clearly.

SUSIE   You can see things more clearly, that's for sure.

GRANDMA   This magnifying glass reminds me of a very special Bible verse, Susie. Psalm 34:3: "Oh, magnify the LORD with me, and let us exalt His name together" (NKJV).

SUSIE   If magnify means to make bigger, how could I magnify the Lord or make him look bigger? He is so big and awesome already.

GRANDMA   You just did magnify the Lord, Susie. When we tell others about how mighty and good the Lord is and all the wonderful things he has done and continues to do, we magnify him. We make him look bigger and mightier to ourselves and others.

SUSIE   So, just like this magnifying glass makes things bigger so I can see things more clearly, people are supposed to magnify the Lord so other people can see him more clearly.

GRANDMA   Right, Susie. On our way home from our hike we can tell all the great things God does for people.

SUSIE   We can magnify the Lord together like your special verse in Psalm 34:3 says, Grandma. This will be great.

GRANDMA   Let's try to think of one great thing about the Lord for each letter of the alphabet.

SUSIE   Okay. I'll start magnifying the Lord with A. He's awesome. *Awesome* starts with A.

GRANDMA   Good. Let's see, the next letter in the alphabet is B. The Lord is big.

SUSIE   *(Pause for a second)* Hmmm.

GRANDMA   Susie, why is it taking you so long to think of a C?

SUSIE   It's not, Grandma, I already have one for C. The Lord is caring. It's taking me a long time because I was trying to think which one of us is going to have to come up with a word that begins with X to describe or magnify the Lord.

GRANDMA   We'll use X-tra special.

SUSIE   Grandma, X-tra special doesn't start with an X.

GRANDMA   We'll keep it our little secret, Susie. I think X-tra special is a good idea.

SUSIE   Me, too. What big ideas you have, Grandma!

GRANDMA   The better to magnify the Lord with you, my dear.

Snow What?

Characters

Boy puppet
Girl puppet
Mom puppet

Props

Charlie and Susie each need to be wearing a cap, scarf, and earmuffs.

(CHARLIE and SUSIE enter with gear on their heads. SUSIE just stands still with muffs on.)

CHARLIE   Mom, Mom!

(MOM comes up.)

MOM   Yes, Charlie.

CHARLIE   Mom, playing in the snow is just great! Can we go back after we eat lunch?

MOM   Sure. We'll have some hot soup and get you all warmed up first.

CHARLIE   Great! I want tomato soup, okay?

MOM   Susie, would tomato soup be okay with you?

(SUSIE doesn't answer, just stands there.)

CHARLIE   You'll have to speak louder. Her brain is frozen. At least today she has an excuse!

MOM   Charlie! *(A little louder to SUSIE)* Susie, would tomato soup be okay with you?

SUSIE   Huh? Mom, I can't hear you.

(SUSIE bends down. Have someone take earmuffs off.)

SUSIE   *(Continues)* What did you say, Mom? I couldn't hear you. Your voice was muffled with these ear muffs. *(SUSIE laughs.)* I'm so funny.

MOM   *(Laughs)* Susie, you amaze me. You truly are one of a kind!

CHARLIE   Mom, that reminds me. John White said his mom told him no two snowflakes are alike. Every snowflake is one of a kind!

SUSIE   Snow what! Get it? So what—snow what.

CHARLIE   *(Groans)* Susie, I liked you better when your brain was frozen.

MOM   Kids! John White's mom is right. There are no two snowflakes alike.

CHARLIE   Wow!

SUSIE   Not even *one* snowflake is the same as another?

MOM   No, Susie, God makes each snowflake different.

CHARLIE   That's something!

MOM   You know what is even greater?

CHARLIE and SUSIE   What?

MOM   God not only makes each snowflake different, he makes every person different. No two persons are ever made the same. Each of us is unique.

SUSIE   Are you sure there are no two people made the same, Mom? What about twins?

MOM   Sometimes people look alike, but God made each person special. No two people are exactly the same. Not even twins.

CHARLIE   Wow! Wait until I tell John White this. He won't believe me.

MOM   Charlie and Susie, do you remember on your birth certificate how there are two little feet and hands?

CHARLIE   Yes. You said they were ours when we were babies.

MOM   Yes, Charlie, every one of those handprints and footprints are different. Policemen use thumbprints and fingerprints to identify people, because each one is different. Every person's thumbprint is unique.

CHARLIE   When we get back out in the snow, I'm going to tell John White.

SUSIE   You mean "Snow" White, don't you? John was all covered with snow the last time I saw him. Get it? Snow White! Ha! Ha!

MOM   Let me share a verse from the Bible and then we'll go get some soup. The verse is in Psalm 119:73: "Thy hands made me and fashioned me" (NASB). God not only made each person but he fashioned each person. He made each person unique.

SUSIE   You mean I'm God's fashion statement! Ha! Ha! Fashion statement— get it?

MOM   Yes, Susie, I've never thought of it that way before, but, yes, each person is especially fashioned by God to be unique. Let's go get our tomato soup.

SUSIE   Maybe we should have split pea soup. We're going to eat soup and split for the snow. Get it? Split pea soup!

(CHARLIE and MOM groan and leave.)

SUSIE   *(While leaving)* My side is *splitting* with laughter. Split pea soup—side splitting. I'm on a roll! Maybe we'll have rolls with our soup. *(Goes off laughing)* God really should have made two of me!

Animals: Be a Friend in the Forest

Characters

Dad puppet
Boy puppet
Girl puppet
Cat puppet
Dog puppet

(CHARLIE and SUSIE appear.)

SUSIE   *(Loudly)* Daaaddd . . . Daaaddd . . .

CHARLIE   Susie! Quiet!

SUSIE   Daaaddd . . . Daaaddd . . .

(DAD appears.)

DAD   My goodness. What is all the noise?

SUSIE   Dad, Charlie is being mean . . . again!

CHARLIE   Am not.

SUSIE   Are too.

DAD   Okay, kids, what's the problem? Did Charlie eat your candy bar or something?

SUSIE   No, Dad, Charlie shot a bird's nest out of the tree with his slingshot!

DAD   Charlie, is that true?

CHARLIE   Well, kind of. Would you believe I was cleaning my slingshot, and it accidentally went off and hit that bird's nest?

DAD   Charlie, I don't think slingshots accidentally go off, do they?

CHARLIE   *(Meekly)* Well, I guess not.

SUSIE   Lucky for you there were no eggs or any birds in the nest, or you would have had big trouble, compliments of Susie Green!

DAD   Now, Susie, what Charlie did was wrong, but that's no way to talk.

CHARLIE   It was just a dumb old bird's nest. What difference does it make?

DAD   Charlie, all the animals God made are important. We shouldn't be mean to any of them or hurt them needlessly, *(Looking at Susie)* and we shouldn't threaten our brothers, either.

CHARLIE   Dad, I know all people are important, *(Looks at Susie)* and we should never threaten them, but I was just having fun.

DAD   It's never fun when harm is being done to one of God's creatures. Listen to Matthew 10:29: "Not one sparrow (What do they cost? Two for a penny?) can fall to the ground without your Father knowing it" (TLB). Our heavenly Father cares for every bird, and every one of his creations.

CHARLIE   You mean every bird is taken care of by God?

DAD   Yes, Charlie, that's right.

SUSIE   Wow! Even I didn't know that!

CHARLIE   What? Something Susie didn't know?

DAD   Now, kids, I think you both could learn something new. God wants you to be kind to all animals and to care for them and their homes, such as bird's nests.

(CALEB and METHUSELAH appear.)

CALEB and METHUSELAH   Bark and Meow. (Nodding heads up and down)

DAD   Looks like Caleb and Methuselah agree!

CHARLIE   You know, it seems all animals are just as important to God as Caleb and Methuselah are to us.

DAD   That's right, only even more so.

CHARLIE   I think I'll be more careful next time I am cleaning my slingshot.

DAD   Yes, Charlie, that would be a good idea.

Let Your Yes Be Yes

Characters

Dad puppet
Mom puppet
Boy puppet
Girl puppet
Dog puppet

(CHARLIE appears, talking to the audience.)

CHARLIE   Wow, I can't believe it. I get to go to Fun World, the greatest amusement park in the state—and for free!

(Move arm up and down like he is riding a roller coaster.)

CHARLIE   We'll ride the roller coaster!

(Move arm in a circular motion.)

CHARLIE   We'll go on the death-defying spinner!

(Move arm to show he is getting hit by other bumper cars.)

CHARLIE   We'll crash in the bumper cars, and we'll eat cotton candy until we turn green.

(MOM and DAD appear.)

MOM   Charlie, what are you so excited about?

CHARLIE   I just got off the phone with Benny, and he invited me to go to Fun World—and for free!

DAD   For free?

CHARLIE   Yes, that's his birthday present this year. His folks said he could ask one friend, and he chose me!

MOM   Charlie, that's wonderful. I know you'll have a good time.

DAD   When are you going?

CHARLIE   Next Saturday.

MOM   But, Charlie, don't you remember what next Saturday is?

CHARLIE   Yes, sure, but I'll just skip it.

DAD   What is next Saturday?

CHARLIE   Oh, it's the youth car wash at church to help raise money for the new organ.

MOM   Charlie, didn't you sign up and tell the director you would be there to help wash cars?

CHARLIE   Yes, but that was before I got invited to Fun World by Benny.

DAD   But, Charlie, didn't you make a commitment to be at the car wash before Benny asked you to go to Fun World?

CHARLIE   Yes, I did, but that doesn't really count when something better comes along.

MOM   But, Charlie, what if all the youth decided not to show up next Saturday? What would happen to the car wash?

CHARLIE   Well, I guess there wouldn't be any. But I'm sure lots of kids will show up.

MOM   Charlie, I think you're missing the point. You made a commitment, and you need to keep your promise.

CHARLIE   I didn't make a promise or anything like that. I just said I'd be there. I didn't give the triple kings X sign or anything like that to make it a real promise.

DAD   Charlie, a verse in the Bible, Matthew 5:37, says, "Say just a simple 'Yes, I will' or 'No, I won't.' Your word is enough" (TLB).

MOM   Charlie, that means when you say you will do something, you will, even if something better comes along.

DAD   Remember two weeks ago when Grandpa and Grandma Green took you and Susie to the zoo, and you saw the new African exhibit?

CHARLIE   Yes, that was great. I'm ready to go again to see the elephants! Do you know how you can tell if an elephant has been in the refrigerator?

MOM   No. How?

CHARLIE   He left his footprint in the jello!

DAD   Okay, let's not get started on your elephant jokes. As I was saying, your grandparents were offered two tickets to see the new musical play in town. Mrs. Brown was sick and couldn't go, so they offered your grandparents the tickets.

CHARLIE   What?

MOM   They turned them down because they had made a commitment to you and Susie to take you to the zoo and didn't want to break their promise.

CHARLIE   Gosh, I know they really wanted to see that new play. They didn't even say anything about it to Susie or me. Boy, I feel bad.

DAD   Charlie, sometimes you will make a commitment to someone and something better will come along, and it's tough to say no.

CHARLIE   I see what you mean. I guess I need to call Benny back and tell him I can't go, because I made a promise to help at the carwash first.

MOM   Yes, son, that's the right thing to do.

DAD   You know, Charlie, your mother and I were talking about taking you and Susie to Fun World sometime in the next few weeks or so. Would you like that?

(SUSIE appears.)

SUSIE   Did I hear someone say Fun World?

(Move arm up and down as if she is riding a roller coaster.)

SUSIE   We'll ride the roller coaster!

(Move arm in a circular motion.)

SUSIE   We'll go on the death-defying spinner!

(Move arm to show she is getting hit by other bumper cars.)

SUSIE   We'll crash the bumper cars.

CHARLIE   You forgot something.

SUSIE   What?

CHARLIE   What about the cotton candy?

SUSIE   Yes, we'll eat cotton candy until we are blue!

CHARLIE   Susie, I think that's green!

SUSIE   Oh, well, I need to go practice my screams for the roller coaster.

CHARLIE   I need to go call Benny.

SUSIE   *(From behind the curtain)* Whee! Ohhhh. . . .

MOM   That's our kids!

DAD   Sure enough! Am I going to get you on the roller coaster this year, dear?

MOM   If you can get our dog, Caleb, to meow instead of bark, I'll go on the roller coaster.

DAD   I get the point, dear. It's impossible to get a dog to meow.

MOM   And it's impossible to get me on a roller coaster.

CHARLIE   *(Comes back with CALEB)* Dad and Mom, guess what new trick I taught Caleb!

DAD   What trick?

CHARLIE   I taught him to meow. I just tell him to talk like Methuselah our cat, and he meows.

DAD   Wow, son, let's see!

CHARLIE   Talk like Methuselah, Caleb.

CALEB   Meow!

DAD   I've got a surprise for you, too, Charlie. Your mom's going on the roller coaster this year with us.

CHARLIE   Wow!

DAD   Remember, dear, let your yes be yes.

CHARLIE   Are you really going, Mom?

MOM   Yes, Charlie, I'm really going on the roller coaster. I've learned a valuable lesson today. Be careful what you say you will do.

CHARLIE   Mom, that was the lesson I learned. I didn't know moms still needed to learn lessons.

MOM   Yes, we all need to keep growing.

CHARLIE   It's a good thing we're the Green family. Green grows better.

Respecting Policemen

Characters

Boy puppet
Girl puppet
Grandpa puppet
Grandma puppet

(CHARLIE and SUSIE appear.)

CHARLIE   I don't either!

SUSIE   You do so!

CHARLIE   Don't either!

SUSIE   Do so!

(GRANDPA and GRANDMA appear.)

GRANDPA   Charlie, Susie! What are you two arguing about?

SUSIE   Charlie got a warning ticket while we were riding our bicycles over here to visit you all. He says he doesn't deserve the ticket.

CHARLIE   Yes, that copper was just wasting the taxpayer's money. Why wasn't he out chasing some real crooks or something?

SUSIE   Charlie, you were breaking the law and almost got hit by a car.

CHARLIE   Big deal! That car missed me by a mile. I gave her a chance to test her brakes. That cop was just picking on me 'cause I'm a kid.

GRANDPA   So, Charlie, you do admit you were breaking the law?

CHARLIE   Well, yes, but it's not an important law, and that so-called policeman is really lame. I've heard this is the only town in the country where the police department has an unlisted phone number.

SUSIE   Charlie Green, that's not true!

CHARLIE   You know, I heard that the cops in this town are so bad they have burglary insurance on the police station.

GRANDPA   Charlie, I think we need to talk. I don't think your attitude towards our police department is very pleasing in God's eyes.

GRANDMA   When you are disobedient or disrespectful to a policeman, you are not following what the Bible says. You are disobeying God.

CHARLIE   Ah, Grandma, the Bible doesn't say anything about policemen, *(Slowly and hesitantly)* does it?

GRANDPA   A verse in the Bible talks about how we should treat policemen, even though it doesn't call them policemen. It calls them our authorities.

CHARLIE   What's an authority, Grandpa?

GRANDPA   Someone God has placed over you to rule you and to care for you—like your folks, teachers, pastors, and policemen.

GRANDMA   Remember last year when Grandpa got his first speeding ticket?

CHARLIE   Yes, I remember.

GRANDMA   What did Grandpa do after getting his speeding ticket?

CHARLIE   He shook the policeman's hand and said, "Thanks for doing your job, sir."

SUSIE   I've never seen a policeman look so surprised!

CHARLIE   Yes, his mouth looked like my goldfish's mouth—gaping open.

GRANDMA   Charlie, Grandpa didn't like getting a ticket, but he knew the policeman was doing his job, and Grandpa needed to respect him.

CHARLIE   Grandpa, what is that verse in the Bible you were telling me about?

GRANDPA   It's in Romans 13:1. Listen to these words: "Let every person be in subjection to the governing authorities. For there is no authority except from God, and those which exist are established by God" (NASB).

CHARLIE   Wow! I guess I have had a bad attitude toward policemen. I didn't know God put them here!

GRANDMA   Remember, Charlie, policemen are there to protect us and help us, not to pick on us.

CHARLIE   I think while I'm here for our visit I'll write a letter to the police and thank them for doing a good job. I could take it down to the police station on my bike ride home. Don't worry, Grandpa and Grandma, I'll be careful to obey all the traffic rules.

GRANDPA   I'm proud of you, Charlie. Your letter will probably make the policeman's day.

SUSIE   Oh! I've heard policemen on T.V. say, "Go ahead—make my day!" I didn't know they meant to write a nice letter.

(EVERYONE starts laughing except SUSIE.)

SUSIE   What's so funny?

CHARLIE   Susie, come help me make my card for the police, and I'll explain it to you. You can help me think of what rhymes with copper.

GRANDMA   Charlie!

CHARLIE   Don't worry, Grandma, I was just kidding.

(CHARLIE and SUSIE leave.)

GRANDPA   *(Laughing)* Those grandkids of mine surely make my day!

Love of Money—Doesn't Make Cents

Characters

Boy puppet
Girl puppet
Mom puppet
Dad puppet

Props

Pretend money.

(CHARLIE comes up with one dollar bills sticking out of his pockets, T-shirt, etc.)

(SUSIE appears.)

CHARLIE   *(Singing)* I'm in the money! I'm in the money!

SUSIE   Charlie, where did you get all that money?

CHARLIE   From my lemonade stand in front of the house.

SUSIE   How much did you make?

CHARLIE   I don't know, but Mr. Bridges, the president of the bank, asked if I could give him a loan. *(Singing)* I'm in the money! I'm in the money!

(MOM appears.)

MOM   Charlie Green, I think we need to have a little talk. I just got off the phone with several of our neighbors.

CHARLIE   Who did you talk with?

MOM   Well, Mrs. Johnson said she asked to buy a glass of your lemonade which was advertised for twenty-five cents. Then when she gave you twenty-five cents, you said it was two dollars and twenty-five cents because you were charging one dollar for the cup and another dollar for the ice!

CHARLIE   Well, I was just trying to be a smart businessman.

MOM   A little later, I talked to Mrs. Smith. She said she gave you a five-dollar bill, and you asked her if you could keep the change!

CHARLIE   Well, she's pretty rich, and I didn't think she would miss the five bucks.

(DAD appears.)

DAD   Charlie, what is that sign in front of our house: "Girls clothing real cheap see Charlie"?

CHARLIE   Well, I need some more money, and I thought I'd sell some of Susie's clothes. She will never miss them.

SUSIE   Sell my clothes!

CHARLIE   Yes, the clothes bar in your closet is about to break in two. I thought I'd get rid of some of your clothes so Dad wouldn't have to reinforce the house under them.

Besides, I got $10.00 for your old blue dress.

SUSIE   You sold my blue dress?

DAD   Charlie, you should not have done that.

CHARLIE   I just don't want to be poor. The only good thing about being poor is that it doesn't cost very much.

DAD   I think you are placing too much emphasis on money. Money can't buy everything. Money can't buy happiness, son.

CHARLIE   I'd sure like to try it!

MOM   Charlie, the Bible speaks a lot about our attitude towards money.

CHARLIE   You're right, Mom. Someone told me, "Money talks," and so far all it's said to me is good-bye.

MOM   Charlie, whoever told you money talks wasn't quoting from the Bible.

CHARLIE   They weren't?

DAD   Listen to a verse from the Bible about money. Hebrews 13:5: "Let your way of life be free from the love of money, being content with what you have" (NASB).

MOM   Charlie, you have many comforts already, and when you love money you put money as being more important than God.

CHARLIE   Than God! I don't want to have anything be more important than God.

DAD   There is nothing wrong with money and having nice things, but when we cheat people to get money or do mean or selfish things just to get money, we are wrong.

SUSIE   Mean things—like selling my blue dress!

DAD   We will talk about that later, Susie.

SUSIE   Until then, Charlie's life is like money. It's worth about five cents.

DAD   Now, Susie.

MOM   Charlie, do you understand what the verse meant that your father read to you?

CHARLIE   I think so, Mom. I should be content with what I have, even if other kids have more; and I should not put such an emphasis on money. It will cause me to cheat or be dishonest . . .

SUSIE   Or mean! . . . and sell your sister's dress!

CHARLIE   You're right, Susie. I should not have sold your dress. I should have sold your black shoes.

SUSIE   What?

CHARLIE   Just kidding, Susie. I'm going to try to buy your ten-dollar dress back, even if I have to pay twenty dollars!

DAD   It sounds like you've learned your lesson.

MOM   Charlie you're a good boy. You're worth a million.

SUSIE   Wow! Maybe I could find a buyer!

DAD   Susie, maybe we need to repeat Hebrews 13:5 to you.

SUSIE   Just teasing, Dad!

Dinosaurs: When, Where, How?

Characters

Grandpa puppet
Boy puppet

(GRANDPA and CHARLIE appear.)

GRANDPA   Hi, Charlie, how was school today?

CHARLIE   Oh, pretty good. I'm kind of confused.

GRANDPA   Are you getting into some more hard math problems?

CHARLIE   No, we are studying dinosaurs.

GRANDPA   Oh, that's an interesting subject.

CHARLIE   Grandpa, I know you are pretty old. Were dinosaurs around when you were a kid?

GRANDPA   *(Chuckling)* Now, Charlie, I'm not quite that old!

CHARLIE   Does the Bible ever say anything about dinosaurs, Grandpa?

GRANDPA   Well, no, it doesn't mention them specifically. But, we do know God made them, because God made all the animals.

CHARLIE   Gosh, I never thought of that!

GRANDPA   Just like God made whales, bears, and all the big animals we see today, he also made the dinosaurs, even though they are extinct.

CHARLIE   My teacher used that word *extinct,* but what does it mean?

GRANDPA   *Extinct* is used for animals who once lived on earth but now are all gone. Some people think dinosaurs became *extinct* before the flood in Noah's time, others think after. No one knows for sure.

CHARLIE   How come the Bible doesn't tell us about dinosaurs?

GRANDPA   Well, Charlie, in the Bible God doesn't tell us everything we want to know, but he does tell us the things we need to know.

CHARLIE   So, I guess we don't really know what happened to all the dinosaurs, and nobody can say for sure.

GRANDPA   That's right, Charlie. All we know is that they lived a long, long time ago.

CHARLIE   I guess God chose not to tell anybody.

GRANDPA   Yes, some things God has just kept to himself. A verse in the Bible which has helped me with things I can't understand is Deuteronomy 29:29: "The secret things belong to the LORD our God, but the things revealed belong to us and to our sons forever" (NASB).

CHARLIE   You mean, God has secrets?

GRANDPA   You could say that, Charlie, but think of all the things he *has* told to us and revealed to us in the Bible.

CHARLIE   You're right, Grandpa. Besides, we don't need to know everything do we?

GRANDPA   No, we don't.

CHARLIE   When we get to heaven, we can ask God.

GRANDPA   That's right. God knows everything.

CHARLIE   One thing I would like to know, Grandpa.

GRANDPA   What's that, Charlie?

CHARLIE   Well, it's my birthday in three days, and that big package in the closet with my name on it from you and Grandma . . .

GRANDPA   Wait a minute! Just as God has secrets, so do I, and that's one of them.

CHARLIE   Aw, shucks!

Our Thoughts—Our Choice

Characters

Boy puppet
Mom puppet

CHARLIE   *(Comes up by himself. He's whistling along and starts singing a happy song.)* It's a happy day and I thank God for the weather. It's a happy day . . . *(He stops and faces audience.)*

CHARLIE   Hmmm *(As if he's thinking)*

CHARLIE   Hmmm *(A little louder and grumpy)*

CHARLIE   *(To himself)* That no-good-for-nothing.

CHARLIE   Huh! I'm so mad. *(Mutters under breath)*

(Starts going back across stage singing)

CHARLIE   It's a crummy day, and I sure hate the weather. It's a crummy day . . .

MOM   *(Comes up. CHARLIE has his head down and bumps into her.)* Charlie, what in the world has made you so grumpy? When you left the breakfast table after family devotions just a couple of minutes ago, you were happy and singing.

CHARLIE   Mom, I got to thinking about the time that no-good-for-nothing John White borrowed my bike without asking and ran over glass and made the tire go flat. I'm in a bad mood now!

MOM   Charlie, that happened a couple of months ago. Why are you thinking about that now?

CHARLIE   Well, it just popped into my mind, and the more I thought about it, the madder I got. Now I'm in a horrible mood, and it's all that John White's fault.

MOM   No, Charlie, I disagree with you. It's not John White's fault you are in a bad mood.

CHARLIE   Well, whose fault is it then?

MOM   It's your fault for choosing to think about something negative like the time John White ruined your tire.

CHARLIE   You mean it's my choice what I think about?

MOM   Thoughts pop into our minds, but we choose to think about them a long time.

CHARLIE   You mean when I thought about John White this morning I shouldn't have thought very long about the bad thing he did?

MOM   Right. John White has done so many good things. You could choose to think about those things. A verse in the Bible, Philippians 4:8, tells people what they should think about. You listen as I tell you this verse and then tell me what people should think about.

CHARLIE   Okay, Mom.

MOM   "Finally, brethren, whatever is true, whatever is honorable, whatever is right, whatever is pure, whatever is lovely, whatever is of good repute, if there is any excellence and if anything worthy of praise, let your mind dwell on these things" (NASB).

CHARLIE   That sure is a lot of things to think about, and they all are good things.

MOM   Right, Charlie. I like the part of the verse that says "dwell on these things." In other words, think long about or concentrate on the good things.

CHARLIE   I wasn't doing that this morning, and I surely ruined my day. You were right, Mom. It wasn't John's fault. It was my fault.

MOM   You can change that and think about good things now. Here, let me tell you a joke to get you laughing again. Did you hear about the man who got fired from the orange-juice factory?

CHARLIE   No, Mom. What happened?

MOM   He couldn't concentrate.

CHARLIE   Oh, Mom, I get it. He couldn't concentrate—concentrated orange juice! That's funny. I think I'll go see if John wants to play. I'll tell him my new joke.

MOM   Remember, Charlie, what you concentrate on or think about is your choice.

CHARLIE   Okay, Mom. *(Goes off singing)* It's a happy day . . .

Reflection

Characters

Girl puppet
Cat puppet
Mom puppet

Props

Mom's blouse or outfit needs red splotches all over the front of it.

SUSIE   *(Talking to METHUSELAH)* Methuselah, I'm so-o-o-o-o embarrassed. You wouldn't believe this family we live in.

(METHUSELAH meows and rubs up against SUSIE, nodding.)

SUSIE   Maybe you would! I went to our neighbors the Whites for their anniversary brunch party, and *Steve Brown* was at the party. He's so cute. Believe me, Methuselah, when I say he's the cat's meow.

METHUSELAH   Meow.

SUSIE   Oh, you've met him?

SUSIE   Well, wouldn't you know, at the party Dad, Mom and Charlie embarrassed me so-o-o-o-o much. Dad was telling one of his jokes, and he had a piece of spinach between his front two teeth. Mom told him, and he went and got it off, but I could

have died! Steve probably thinks our family is awful. And, then, Methuselah, you won't believe it. Mom! She was eating a jelly donut while everyone, including the handsome Steve Brown, was in the room, and guess what, Methuselah! Mom took a bite out of her jelly donut on the wrong side, and all the jelly squirted out the other side all over her bright yellow blouse—red jelly everywhere. Can you believe it, Methuselah? I wanted to crawl in a hole somewhere and never come out!

METHUSELAH   *(Meows sympathetically)*

SUSIE   Methuselah, you wouldn't believe what Charlie did! The younger guys were playing tackle football in the backyard. Charlie was running to tackle wonderful Steve, who had the ball, and missed. He ran into the White's new fence and knocked part of the fence down. Steve probably can't believe it. I have a brother who tackles fences! And then to top it all off, Methuselah, Caleb, Charlie's dog, came through the hole in the fence and jumped up on the buffet table and started eating the ham. Methuselah, I am ruined—a has-been, and it's all because of my family!

MOM   *(Comes up)* There you are, Susie. We missed you at the party, and I thought I had better come and see if you were okay. (Looks down.) I needed to change my blouse, anyway. Can you believe this happened? It was so funny.

SUSIE   Mom, I didn't think it was funny. I was embarrassed. Our whole family embarrassed me, and I came home.

MOM   Susie, I'm sorry these things happened, but, honey, you are making things worse by coming home and sulking.

SUSIE   What do you mean, Mom. How can I make things any worse? They are awful.

MOM   Susie, you left Pam White all alone. She has no one to play with her. You had told her you would be at the party, and now you are not there to play with her. How do you think the Whites will feel when they find out you left their party?

SUSIE   They would probably feel pretty badly, huh?

MOM   Susie, I think you could learn a valuable lesson from this.

SUSIE   You mean, change my last name from Green?

MOM   Susie Marie Green!

SUSIE   I'm sorry, Mom. What lesson were you talking about?

MOM   You know how you feel when our family has had some embarrassing things happen?

SUSIE   Sure, Mom, I know.

MOM   Well, just as our family reflects on you, so each person who is God's child reflects on God. A person who becomes a Christian is part of God's family.

SUSIE   You mean, every person who is a Christian is a part of God's family?

MOM   Yes. Jesus, while he was here on earth, said, "For whoever does the will of God, he is My brother and sister and mother" (Mark 3:35 NASB).

SUSIE   Wow! Christians reflect on God.

MOM   People need to be careful how they act when they know Jesus.

SUSIE   People need to be more concerned about their reflection on God.

MOM   Right, Susie. Oh, I forgot to tell you. Bobby Black was asking where you were.

SUSIE   The hunk, Bobby Black, was asking about me! Wow! I'm in love! Bobby Black. (Runs off, saying) I'd better hurry back to the party.

MOM   (Shaking her head) I thought she was in love with Steve Brown this morning. Methuselah, sometimes I worry about this family.

(METHUSELAH rubs up against MOM, nods, and meows.)

But, Mom, It's Not Fair—He Gets To . . .

Characters

Boy puppet
Girl puppet
Mom puppet

_____

(CHARLIE, SUSIE and MOM all come up)

CHARLIE   Well, I'm off to ride my bike over to John White's house. *(CHARLIE leaves.)*

SUSIE   That's not fair, Mom. You won't let me ride my bike that far.

MOM   Susie, Charlie is older than you.

SUSIE   I hate those words! Older, smolder! He always gets to do everything, and I don't get to do anything just because I'm younger.

MOM   Susie, that's not true.

SUSIE   Uh-huh! He gets to stay up a whole half-hour later than me. He gets a quarter more allowance than me. He gets everything, and I get nothing. IT'S JUST NOT FAIR!

MOM   Susie, if you keep acting like this, you will not get to do these things you are wanting to do. You need to show your father and me that you deserve to be able to do more. If you act like a baby, you can only do baby things.

SUSIE   I'm sorry, Mom. I'm going to try to act better and show you and Dad I am growing up.

MOM   That's my girl!

SUSIE   Mom, I'm not a girl!

MOM   That's my young lady!

MOM   Susie, Charlie also has more responsibility because he's older. Your father and I expect more from him, such as doing more things around the house. Do you remember last night when he wanted to go play with his friends, and we told him he couldn't because he had to be with you while we went to the neighbors for a visit?

SUSIE   Yes, he told me he hated being older. It's so much work. I see what you mean, Mom. It is more responsibility.

MOM   You need to be glad right now for what you can do. Remember, Dad just let you start staying up a little longer on your last birthday.

SUSIE   Yes, but I also had to start taking out the trash!

MOM   Right! Remember, with privileges come responsibility.

SUSIE   All this talk about work, I'm getting tired. I think I'll go play. That's one great thing about being a kid.

MOM   That's right. You have plenty of time to grow up. Enjoy right now.

CHARLIE   *(Comes up)* I forgot my water bottle for my bike.

MOM   I'm glad. You and Susie come here for a minute. We forgot to have our Bible reading at breakfast this morning, and I want to share a verse with you both. It's John 21:21–22: "Peter therefore seeing him said to Jesus, 'Lord and what about this man?' Jesus said to him, 'If I want him to remain until I come, what is that to you? You follow me!'" (NASB).

CHARLIE   Who was Peter asking the Lord about?

MOM   Peter was asking Jesus about John, another disciple.

SUSIE   Kind of like me asking you about Charlie?

MOM   Right, Susie. Jesus told Peter to concentrate on himself and not be so concerned about what Jesus was asking John to do.

CHARLIE   Last night I needed to concentrate on obeying you and Dad when you wanted me to stay with Susie instead of complaining about Susie being young and me having to take care of her because I was older.

MOM   Good, you kids understand. Charlie, did you get your dusting done this morning?

CHARLIE   I forgot. I'll do it now.

SUSIE   Well, I am going to play. It's easy being young!

(CHARLIE and MOM look at each other, laugh, and go down.)

Why Pray When You Can Worry?

Characters

Girl puppet
Boy puppet
Mom puppet

SUSIE   *(Comes in and starts pacing back and forth across the stage, muttering to herself)* What am I going to do? What in the world is going to happen? What if I don't get one? What will I do? I just know I'm not going to get one. Maybe I will get one—no, I doubt it! I can't stand this stress! *(SUSIE bumps into MOM.)*

MOM   Susie, what are you mumbling about?

SUSIE   I'm talking to myself. I'm not mumbling. You said mumbling was not speaking loud enough so people could hear. I couldn't be mumbling, because I can hear myself fine.

MOM   Well, what are you talking to yourself about?

SUSIE   Jenny, the most popular girl in our class, is having a birthday party next week, and she sent out the invitations yesterday. I was worrying that I might not get an invitation. Then what would I do, Mom?

MOM   Not go to the party?

SUSIE   I mean if I don't get an invitation to her party, it will be awful.

CHARLIE   *(Comes up and looks down. Move his head back and forth as he says his line.)* Why is there this path in the floor?

MOM   Susie is pacing while she waits for the mail.

SUSIE   I'm worried about not getting an invitation to Jenny's birthday party. *(Starts pacing)*

CHARLIE   Don't *worry* about it, Susie! I hear the mailman coming. I'll go get the mail. *(Leaves)*

SUSIE   Oh, no, I'm so worried I can't look.

MOM   Susie, let's have a talk while Charlie goes for the mail.

SUSIE   What's on your mind?

MOM   I'm concerned about what's on your mind, Susie. All this worrying is not good for you. Do you remember the verse you memorized last Sunday for Sunday school?

SUSIE   Sure. Philippians 4:6: "Be anxious for nothing, but in everything by prayer and supplication with thanksgiving let your requests be made known to God" (NASB).

MOM   *Anxious* means to worry.

SUSIE   Then we're to worry about nothing. That verse couldn't mean worrying about invitations to birthday parties. This is important.

MOM   Susie, it says to worry about nothing, and that means birthday parties.

SUSIE   But what's a girl to do?

MOM   The rest of your verse tells you. You are supposed to pray about what worries you, and thank God.

SUSIE   But how can I thank God? I don't know if I have the invitation yet.

MOM   Susie, a person prays about her problem or concern and then thanks God he is going to take care of it in the way he knows best. We are to trust God and not worry.

SUSIE   I see, Mom. I kind of wasted this whole morning.

MOM   That's right, Susie. Worrying is a waste.

SUSIE   Next time I want to worry, I'll remember to pray and thank God.

(CHARLIE comes in.)

CHARLIE   Susie got a letter from Jenny.

SUSIE   Wow! Super!

MOM   Susie, one more lesson. Most of the things we waste time worrying about never happen anyway.

SUSIE   You're right, Mom! But what will I wear to the party? I'm worried I won't wear the right thing. Mom, can you pray about what to wear to a party?

MOM   You can pray about anything. Anything that concerns you, concerns God.

SUSIE   Right. Worry about nothing.

MOM   Come on, Susie. We'll go look for a gift for Jenny. *(BOTH leave.)*

CHARLIE   Women! Worrying about invitations, clothes. Why don't they worry about important things, like whether my team is going to win our football game tomorrow?

The Perils of Being Good

Characters

Boy puppet
Girl puppet
Dad puppet

Optional Prop

Square of cardboard on Susie's hand the size of remote control; a puppet hand mover

(CHARLIE and SUSIE are staring ahead as they watch T.V.)

SUSIE   That was a good T.V. show. I always like those Charlie Brown cartoons.

CHARLIE   Yes, I always feel sorry for poor Charlie Brown. He tries so hard. I feel like him sometimes. I feel like my name should be Charlie Brown instead of Charlie Green.

SUSIE   I love Lucy.

CHARLIE   We're not watching "I Love Lucy."

SUSIE   No, silly Charlie. I was saying I like Lucy in the Charlie Brown cartoon.

CHARLIE   She's so mean to Charlie Brown sometimes.

SUSIE   I know. I think it's great.

CHARLIE   Susie, turn off the T.V. now. Dad and Mom said we were to watch only the Charlie Brown special and then turn the T.V. off.

SUSIE   Aren't you a Mister Goodie-Two-Shoes? I'm going to watch this next show.

CHARLIE   Susie, you're going to get in trouble for disobeying.

SUSIE   Be quiet, Mr. Know-It-All. Dad and Mom will never know. They're in the kitchen visiting with the next-door neighbors.

CHARLIE   Well, I'm going to leave.

SUSIE   Aren't you a Mr. Doodle-De-Do-Right. Charlie's a Mr. Doodle-De-Do-Right. Charlie's a Mr. Doodle-De-Do-Right.

CHARLIE   Good-bye, Susie. I'm going to my room.

(CHARLIE starts to leave.)

SUSIE   Bye, Mr. Doodle-De-Do-Right.

DAD   *(Comes in)* Susie, you are watching the T.V. show that Mom and I told you not to watch. You are disobeying us. We told you to turn the T.V. off after the Charlie Brown special.

SUSIE   But, Dad . . .

DAD Susie, I'm disappointed in you. Now go to your room, and I'll be there in a minute. *(SUSIE leaves.)*

CHARLIE Dad, I was just leaving.

DAD I know, son. I heard Susie calling you a Mr. Doodle-De-Do-Right.

CHARLIE Sometimes, Dad, it's hard to do what's right. The kids at school call you Teacher's Pet, and you get called stupid names.

DAD It is hard. I was just reading this morning in my Bible Isaiah 59:15: "And he who turns aside from evil makes himself a prey" (NASB).

CHARLIE You mean when you don't do what's bad, you're a prey? What's it mean to be a prey though, Dad?

DAD When you do good, people who are not doing good feel they are bad and want you to do what's wrong, so they call you names or try to talk you into doing what's wrong so they won't feel they are so bad.

CHARLIE Grandma always says misery loves company. It sounds like people doing bad love company.

DAD It's funny, but people, when they are doing wrong, can't stand to see someone doing good.

CHARLIE Dad, our Sunday school lesson this week was about Cain and Abel. Our teacher told us in the Bible in 1 John 3:12 it says Cain killed his brother Abel because Cain's deeds were evil and Abel's deeds were good.

DAD That's exactly right. Abel was doing good, and Cain was jealous because he wasn't doing good, so he killed Abel.

CHARLIE It is hard sometimes when you do good.

DAD Just remember, son, it's hard sometimes when you do good, but it is the best. Now I need to go decide on Susie's punishment for disobeying. She has disobeyed three times today. Charlie, why don't you go to the kitchen and have pie and ice cream with Mom and the new neighbors. I'll be down in a few minutes. *(DAD leaves.)*

CHARLIE It looks like Susie is going to find out it's not good to be bad and disobey. Pie and ice cream, here I come. Sometimes it's wonderful to be good and obey.

Honesty the Best Policy?

Characters

Boy puppet
Girl puppet
Dad puppet
Mom puppet
Grandpa puppet
Grandma puppet

SUSIE   *(Comes up speaking to herself)* Well, Sunday school is over. That was a pretty interesting lesson today on being honest. I'm going to do like the teacher says and tell the truth. No more lies! Just call me Honest Susie!

CHARLIE   *(Comes up and looks around)* Who are you talking to, Susie?

SUSIE   Myself. I'm much more interesting than you, Charlie. When it comes to listening to you, you're so boring.

CHARLIE   Susie, that's not very nice.

SUSIE   No, Charlie, but I'm just being honest.

(CHARLIE leaves.)

(GRANDMA appears.)

GRANDMA   Hi, Susie, do you like my new dress?

SUSIE   Well, I really don't. If you had stayed on that diet, it would look a lot better. I hope I don't get fat when I'm your age, Grandma.

(GRANDMA leaves.)

(GRANDPA appears.)

GRANDPA   Hi, Susie, how are you?

SUSIE   I'm fine, Grandpa. What have you been up to?

GRANDPA   Not much this week. About the only thing I did was to get a haircut.

SUSIE   With your bald head, I'm sure the barber only charged you half-price. Does he have to wear sunglasses when he cuts your few hairs because of the glare off your head?

GRANDPA   *(Slowly)* Well, no, he doesn't, Susie.

SUSIE   I have just the song to describe your bald head: "Precious and Few."

(GRANDPA leaves.)

(DAD enters.)

DAD   Hey, Susie, how was Sunday school?

SUSIE   Well, not too bad. Except for Miss Johnson, our teacher, who talks funny, and that lame brain Jerry, it was real good.

DAD   Susie, it sounds as if you are being rather critical.

SUSIE   No, Dad, I'm just being honest! We learned about it in Sunday school. I told Charlie he was boring, Grandma she was fat, and Grandpa and I talked about his bald head.

(MOM appears.)

MOM   Hi, what's going on with my favorite daughter and my handsome husband?

SUSIE   Oh, Mom, Dad's not that handsome. On a scale of one to ten, he might be a five or so. I'm the one with all the good looks in the family—a perfect ten.

MOM   Now, Susie! Your father is very handsome! He was the most handsome young man I'd ever seen—those black wiggly eyes, and that gorgeous watermelon-green skin. Well, he still is handsome, Susie Green.

DAD   I think Susie may have misunderstood part of her Sunday school lesson.

SUSIE   I was just being honest, like the Bible says to be!

MOM   So that's the problem.

DAD   Yes, dear, I think so.

MOM   Susie, being honest is telling the truth, but sometimes there are things which don't have to be said.

SUSIE   You mean I shouldn't have called Charlie boring, even if he is sometimes, and I shouldn't have called Grandma fat and Grandpa bald?

DAD   I think you're getting the point.

MOM   The Bible has a verse which might help you—Ephesians 4:15: "But speak(ing) the truth in love" (NASB). Love and honesty need to guide all we decide to say.

DAD   Susie, all of us have faults and shortcomings, but we don't need to focus on them. When Grandma asked how her dress looked, you could have told her it looked just fine on her, or that you liked the color and not mention it might look better if Grandma were a few pounds lighter.

MOM   If someone asks us if we did a certain thing or went to a certain place, we always need to answer with a specific yes or no. But if a person asks for our opinion, we need to answer in a kind and loving way, even if we don't like it 100 percent.

SUSIE   I think I get it. We're never supposed to tell a lie, but sometimes we don't have to say everything we think.

DAD   You're right, Susie.

SUSIE   I think I might need to go and talk to Grandma and Grandpa.

MOM   That would be nice, Susie.

DAD   Susie, don't you think there is someone else you need to talk to?

SUSIE   Well, I forgot . . . Oops, now that is not being honest. I'll look up Charlie first.

MOM and DAD   Good girl!

The Golden Rule Part 2

Characters

Boy puppet
Girl puppet
Mom puppet

Props

Two cardboard or paper boomerangs. Optional prop: a referee shirt for Mom. It's pretty easy if she has on white. Just tape black construction paper strips on her shirt.

(CHARLIE and SUSIE both come up. CHARLIE is whistling, and they are both just looking around.)

CHARLIE   Susie, you surely look ugly today. What happened? Did you sleep on the waffle iron?

SUSIE   Charlie, I am not ugly. I am a sister of the ugliest brother in the world. I got all the good looks in our family.

CHARLIE   What did you do with them, throw them in the trash? You surely didn't keep any good looks for yourself.

(CHARLIE bumps up against SUSIE.)

(SUSIE bumps back.)

(CHARLIE hits SUSIE.)

(SUSIE hits back.)

CHARLIE   Susie, you're a bird brain!

SUSIE   Well, at least I have a brain!

(CHARLIE hits SUSIE.)

(SUSIE hits back.)

(You can have CHARLIE and SUSIE say or do what you like, depending on your puppet capabilities, i.e., stick out tongue, etc. Just have CHARLIE do it first and SUSIE respond in kind. They start fighting.)

MOM   *(Comes up with referee shirt on)* All right, you two. Stop this fighting. We are not going to have any more of this fighting. I'm beginning to understand why Mrs. White gave me this referee shirt when I had my second child. I never thought I would need it. I'm disappointed in you both. Now go to your rooms for time-out. I'll be up in a minute.

(ALL THREE go down. Charlie comes up after a couple of seconds and has a boomerang taped to his hand. Move hand with hand mover like he's playing with it. MOM comes up.)

MOM   Charlie, did you start the fight with your sister?

CHARLIE   Well, kind of. I said something to her, and she said something back. I bumped up against her, and she bumped back. I said something to her, and she said something back. I hit her; she hit me back, and then the fight kind of got started.

MOM   Charlie, I want to share a lesson with you that may really help you. I'm going to use your new boomerang as an example.

CHARLIE   It's fun, because when I throw it, it comes back to me.

MOM   That is exactly what happened downstairs. When you said something ugly to Susie, she said something ugly back. When you hit her, she hit you back. Charlie, just like your boomerang returns to you, so do unkind and ugly things we do to others.

CHARLIE   I see, Mom. When you say ugly things, people say ugly things back. It returns to you.

MOM   Charlie, the good thing about this is that good things and good words come back, also.

CHARLIE   You mean, if I had been nice to Susie downstairs and said something nice, she would have been nice to me back?

MOM   Yes. The Bible talks about this same thing. Let's call it the boomerang effect.

CHARLIE   What are some verses that show the boomerang effect, Mom?

MOM   In the Book of Obadiah God says in verse 15 concerning judgment: "As you have done, it will be done to you. Your dealings will return on your own head" (NASB). Galatians 6:7 says, "Whatsoever a man sows, this he will also reap" (NASB).

CHARLIE   This means if I want people to be nice to me, I need to be nice. If I want people to be mean, I should be mean.

MOM   Right.

CHARLIE   Mom, I want people to be nice to me.

MOM   I know, Charlie. People do not always return back good for good and evil for evil, but usually they do. So you start doing and saying good things, and you watch. Just like that boomerang, they will come back to you.

CHARLIE   Mom, you can get rid of your referee shirt. I'm going to start saying good things to Susie.

MOM   Good boy. During the rest of your time-out I want you to trace your boomerang on a piece of paper and write on the paper all the good things you can think of about Susie. Then you can cut out the boomerang and give it to her.

CHARLIE   Okay, Mom.

SUSIE   (Comes in with boomerang on her hand) Mom, here is a boomerang with nice things written on it for Charlie.

CHARLIE   Thanks, Susie. In just a minute I'll have a return boomerang.

SUSIE   Wow, Mom, you were right! Good things do come back.

MOM   I think things will be a lot safer around here with all these kind things flying around instead of those ugly things I heard and saw this morning.

(ALL THREE leave, and there is a crash off-stage. Puppets continue dialogue from off-stage.)

CHARLIE   Oops—Mom, boomerangs don't always come back.

(Another identical crash.)

CHARLIE   Never mind, Mom, it came back.

MOM   I just thought it was going to be safer around here.

Pitting Parents Against Each Other Is the Pits

Characters

Dad puppet
Mom puppet
Boy puppet
Girl puppet

(CHARLIE and SUSIE appear.)

CHARLIE   Boy, I'm dying for an ice cream cone!

SUSIE   Me, too!

CHARLIE   I want a double dip.

SUSIE   I want a triple dip.

(CHARLIE speaks to audience and talks as if he is speaking under his breath.)

CHARLIE   Somehow a triple dip seems to fit her.

SUSIE   What did you say, Charlie?

CHARLIE   Ah, . . . a triple dip is what I'd like for sure.

SUSIE   Oh, that's what I thought you said!

CHARLIE   The problem is, I'm broke. How about you?

SUSIE   I've got fifteen cents.

CHARLIE   That might buy us the cone but no ice cream.

(DAD appears.)

CHARLIE   Hey, Dad, can we have enough money to get a small ice cream cone at the drugstore?

DAD   Well, maybe. I don't want you kids to spoil your dinner. Go ask your mother what time dinner is. If she says it's okay, then it's okay with me.

CHARLIE and SUSIE   Okay, Dad!

(DAD goes offstage.)

CHARLIE and SUSIE   Mom!

(MOM appears.)

MOM   Did you kids need me?

CHARLIE   Mom, Dad said we could have an ice cream cone, but we have to get the money from you.

SUSIE   Yes, and I think he said we could both have triple dips.

MOM   That doesn't sound like your father since dinner is only in a half-hour; but if he said so, it's okay. Let's go find my purse.

(ALL PUPPETS disappear.)

(CHARLIE and SUSIE come back up.)

133

CHARLIE   Ohhh . . . I feel sick.

SUSIE   Me, too. I never knew a triple dip was so big.

CHARLIE   Me, neither. I feel gross.

(MOM calls from backstage.)

MOM   Charrrlie . . . Susssiiiee. . . . Dinnnner . . .

CHARLIE and SUSIE   Oh, no!

(MOM and DAD appear.)

MOM   Come on, kids. I have a great dinner planned. It's a new recipe, and I know you will love it. I've worked all afternoon.

CHARLIE   Mom, I don't think I can eat a bite.

SUSIE   Me, neither, Mom. We don't feel good!

DAD   What's wrong with you kids? Are you getting a touch of the flu?

CHARLIE   I think we ate too much ice cream.

DAD   Mother, why did you let them have ice cream cones this close to dinner, even if they were just small ones?

MOM   Well, you are the one who told them they could have ice cream cones—triple dippers to boot!

DAD   I told them to check with you since it was so close to dinner.

(CHARLIE and SUSIE start to disappear behind the screen.)

MOM   But I thought you said . . .

(CHARLIE and SUSIE are gone.)

MOM   Charlie!

DAD   Susie!

(CHARLIE and SUSIE appear.)

DAD   Charlie, Susie, I think you have some explaining to do. I didn't say you could have ice cream. I said to check with your mom.

CHARLIE   Ah, well, er . . .

MOM   Kids, I think you lied to me.

SUSIE   Well, er, ah . . . It wasn't exactly a lie . . . I don't think.

DAD   Kids, when you misrepresent the truth or only tell part of the story, that is the same as a lie; and I know you understand what the Bible says about lying.

CHARLIE   *(Slowly)* Yes, we do. We should never lie.

SUSIE   I didn't really think of that as lying.

CHARLIE and SUSIE   We're sorry.

MOM   I think you have learned a good lesson. You should never pit one of your parents against the other.

DAD   And you should always tell the whole truth.

SUSIE   You're right, Mom.

CHARLIE   You're right, Dad.

MOM   *(Looking at Dad)* Dear, do you think we should punish them?

DAD   Honey, I think they have punished themselves.

MOM   You're right, they do look awfully green. Come on. You and I will eat the *good* food.

CHARLIE and SUSIE   Very funny, Mom!

God's Creation

Characters

Boy puppet
Dad puppet

Prop

This sketch takes place at night or dusk. You can give the idea by dimming the lights. If your stage is in front of a wall, you can put up a strip of dark blue or black paper to cover the wall. You need stars for Dad and Charlie to look at (or you can just pretend they are looking at stars). Cotton balls on the dark paper work great. If you have time to do the work, you can cut stars out of aluminum foil. If the wall is white behind the dark paper, you can just punch holes in the paper and give the effect of stars. If your ceiling is not too high, you could even put the paper and stars on the ceiling and have Charlie and Dad look up.

Pair of sunglasses for Charlie.

CHARLIE   *(Comes up with sunglasses on)* I can't see! I can't see! Help, Dad! I can't see. *(Turn head all around as if he is trying to see.)*

DAD   No wonder you can't see. It's night, and you have on your new sunglasses.

CHARLIE   I hear you, Dad, but I can't see you.

DAD   Charlie, why do you have your sunglasses on?

CHARLIE   Well, Dad, you said my new sunglasses were for our camping trip, and we're on our camping trip, so I put them on.

DAD   I meant for you to wear them during the day while we were fishing to keep the sun out of your eyes. Take off the sunglasses, and you'll be able to see better.

CHARLIE   *(Bends down and takes off the glasses. Be sure to put his hand behind the stage so it looks like CHARLIE is taking off the glasses.)* Oh! I see! (Looks around)

DAD   Charlie, look at the beautiful sky.

CHARLIE   Wow! It is beautiful, isn't it, Dad?

DAD   I am so glad God created this beautiful sky and world for us to enjoy.

CHARLIE   Me, too, Dad! What did things look like before God created the world?

DAD   You can shut your eyes and see what it looked like.

CHARLIE   You mean it was all black and dark like when I had my sunglasses on a minute ago?

DAD   Yes, Charlie, the Bible says in Genesis 1:1–2, "In the beginning God created the heavens and the earth. And the earth was formless and void, and darkness was over the surface of the deep" (NASB).

CHARLIE   Everything was dark before God created the world?

DAD   That's right, Charlie.

CHARLIE   Boy, I'm surely glad God created the heavens and this beautiful sky with stars and the moon.

DAD   I like the verse in Psalm 19:1 that says, "The heavens are telling of the glory of God; and the firmament is declaring the work of His hands" (NASB).

CHARLIE   Wow! That's so neat. We really can see the work of God's hands clearly in this beautiful sky tonight, huh, Dad?

DAD   Yes, son. This is wonderful being here with you enjoying God's beautiful sky.

CHARLIE   Dad, I really like this camping out in God's creation in the woods, surviving, just the two of us guys.

(Hooting noise offstage. CHARLIE jumps close to DAD.)

CHARLIE   What's that?

DAD   That's an owl, another part of God's creation. No need to be scared!

CHARLIE   Oh! I wasn't scared, Dad. I just wanted to be close to you.

DAD   *(Laughs)* "Owl" be right here!

The Bible—God's Valentine to Us

Characters

Boy puppet
Girl puppet
Grandpa puppet
Grandma puppet

Props

Two valentines with double-stick tape on back

SUSIE   Charlie! Oh, Charlieeee! Charlie got a valentine from Tammy Smith! Oh, Charlie! *(Hold it up in front of her nose. Use hand holder.)* Mm-m-m-m, smell this valentine. O de de channel 5.

CHARLIE   Give that to me, Susie.

SUSIE   *(Smells valentine again)* I wonder why she didn't use *"CHARLIE"* perfume, since her valentine was for you, CHARLIE!

CHARLIE   It's mine, Susie. Give it to me.

SUSIE   *(Puts valentine behind her back)* Charlie and Tammy, sittin' in a tree, K-I-S-S-I-N-G. First comes love and then comes marriage, and then comes Tammy with a baby carriage.

CHARLIE   Susie, that's mine. Now give it here!

SUSIE   No way. I'm going to read it.

CHARLIE   You'd better not.

GRANDMA   *(Comes up)* Kids, what's going on here?

CHARLIE   Grandma, Susie has my valentine from Tammy Smith and won't give it to me.

SUSIE   I want to read it first.

CHARLIE   No way.

GRANDPA   *(Comes up)* What's going on here?

GRANDMA   Susie has a valentine of Charlie's and won't give it to him.

GRANDPA   Well, I'll tell you what. Susie, you give Charlie his valentine and I'll give you this one addressed to you.

SUSIE   A valentine for me! Wow! Who is it from? I can't wait to read it. Here, Charlie. *(Take valentine off Susie's hand and put on Charlie's behind screen and throw arm over.)*

GRANDPA   Here you go, Susie. *(Make exchange behind screen again.)*

(CHARLIE and SUSIE start to run off.)

GRANDMA   Wait a minute, kids. Where are you going?

CHARLIE and SUSIE   *(Impatiently)* To read our valentines.

GRANDMA   That surprises me.

CHARLIE   Why, Grandma? Everyone loves to read letters.

SUSIE   Yes, especially from someone they love! Like Tammy!

GRANDMA   Well, I have seen a love letter to both of you in your rooms this week while Grandpa and I have been taking care of you. When I was dusting, I had to dust off both of your love letters.

CHARLIE   No way! I must not have seen it.

SUSIE   Where is my love letter?

GRANDMA   I was talking about your love letters from God. Your Bibles.

(CHARLIE and SUSIE sheepishly look down.)

CHARLIE   I've been so busy lately.

GRANDPA   Too busy to read a love letter from someone who loves you?

CHARLIE   You're right, Grandpa.

GRANDPA   How do you think God feels when people don't read his letter to them—the Bible?

SUSIE   Disappointed. I would feel hurt if I wrote you and Grandma a letter and you never read it.

GRANDMA   Exactly, Susie.

GRANDPA   Why don't you both pick out a verse about love to read tonight at supper, since it's Valentine's Day.

GRANDMA   That's a good idea. Why don't all four of us do it. Grandpa, you're so smart. *(Kisses Grandpa on his head)*

CHARLIE   Grandpa, did you ever send Grandma a love letter?

GRANDPA   Yep! I sure did. Spent a lot of time courtin' this pretty thing!

GRANDMA   And believe me, I couldn't wait to read them! Just like I can't wait to read my Bible every morning.

CHARLIE   Me too—now. *(Leaves)*

SUSIE   Thanks, Grandpa and Grandma. *(Leaves)*

GRANDMA   *(Looks at Grandpa)* Do you remember how you used to nibble on my ear, Grandpa?

GRANDPA   *(Starts to leave)* Yep, yep, I sure do remember how I used to nibble on your ear.

GRANDMA   Where are you going?

GRANDPA   To get my teeth!

Christmas—The Real Gift

Characters

Boy puppet
Girl puppet
Grandpa puppet

Optional Props

Santa-type hats for Charlie and Susie

(CHARLIE and SUSIE appear, talking to each other.)

CHARLIE   Wow! Did you see all the packages under the Christmas tree?

SUSIE   Yes, I did! And I think at least half of all the presents are for me!

CHARLIE   No way!

SUSIE   Yes sireeee!

CHARLIE   Well, I've got the biggest one!

SUSIE   Well, I've got more!

(GRANDPA appears.)

GRANDPA   Now children, what is all the noise?

CHARLIE and SUSIE   It's Christmas!

GRANDPA   Yes, Christmas is such a wonderful time!

CHARLIE   Yes, presents and more presents . . .

SUSIE   And more presents!

GRANDPA   My, my, children.

SUSIE   Grandpa, I just want practical gifts this year, like school supplies and . . . a coat with a fur collar . . .

CHARLIE   Yes, and I want a trickmaster bike, and an electric train, and a new fishing pole, and a trampoline . . .

SUSIE   And a huge gift certificate to the department store and . . .

GRANDPA   Slow down, kids. I think you have missed the point of Christmas. Why do we give gifts?

CHARLIE   So kids can get lots of new toys, and a baseball glove, and a football, and a . . .

SUSIE   And a new dress with matching shoes, and a . . .

GRANDPA   Children, that's not the real reason why we give gifts.

CHARLIE and SUSIE   What?

GRANDPA   Charlie, Susie, we give gifts for two reasons.

SUSIE   What are those, Grandpa?

GRANDPA   Well, one is because the wise men came to Jesus and gave him gifts of gold, frankincense, and myrrh.

CHARLIE   Yes, I know about the wise guys! I was one in last year's Christmas play at church.

SUSIE   Charlie, that's wise men, not wise guys.

CHARLIE   Oh, *right,* Susie. What's the other reason, Grandpa?

GRANDPA   Well, we give gifts to cause us to remember that God gave us the best gift of all: the Lord Jesus Christ. Kids, listen to this verse from the Bible that talks about God sending Jesus, 2 Corinthians 9:15: "Thanks be unto God for His indescribable gift" (NASB).

SUSIE   You mean we give gifts to remind us of the wise men giving gifts to the baby Jesus and because God gave us the gift of Jesus?

GRANDPA   That's right, Susie!

CHARLIE   Boy, I guess I kind of missed the point. I just want some more neat toys and clothes.

GRANDPA   Kids, there is nothing wrong with getting and giving gifts, but we need to remember why, and we shouldn't be selfish.

CHARLIE   I gave Dad a list of ten things I wanted for Christmas. Maybe I should tell him I just would like two or three at the most.

SUSIE   Yes, poor Dad. Last year when he was singing a solo at church, instead of singing "I heard the bells on Christmas day," he sang "I heard the bills on Christmas day."

CHARLIE   I guess we can get carried away spending money and miss the real meaning of Christmas. Hey, Grandpa, do you know how to stop a charging elephant at Christmas time?

GRANDPA   I don't know, Charlie.

CHARLIE   Cut up his credit cards. Ha! Ha! Ha!

GRANDPA and SUSIE   Ohhhhh. . . .

SUSIE   Grandpa, I think Charlie was right. He was one of the wise guys.

GRANDPA   I think that may be true, Susie!

Thanksgiving

Characters

Boy puppet
Girl puppet
Mom puppet

(MOM and SUSIE come up.)

MOM   Susie, I'm looking forward to the Thanksgiving play tonight at church. Your Pilgrim outfit is cute. You're going to make a wonderful Pilgrim.

SUSIE   If I can just get Charlie to stop saying *(deep voice)* "Howdy, Pilgrim" every time he sees me.

MOM   I think he's been watching too many John Wayne movies on T.V. lately.

SUSIE   Mom, can you listen to the verse I am saying in the play?

MOM   Sure. I think I know it by now, I've heard it so many times.

SUSIE   I'm sorry, Mom. I'm just so nervous for the play. I've never been a Pilgrim before.

MOM   Oh, Susie, I wasn't complaining. I never tire of hearing you say Bible verses. I just meant I wouldn't need to get my Bible to check and make sure you were saying your verse right.

SUSIE   Here goes. James 1:17: "Every good thing bestowed and every perfect gift is from above, coming down from the Father of lights, with whom there is no variation, or shifting shadow" (NASB).

MOM   Word-perfect, Susie. Now why don't you tell me what it means.

SUSIE   Oh, Mom! We don't have to know what it means. We only have to memorize it and say it in the play.

MOM   That's not a very good attitude about your Bible verse.

SUSIE   It's so hard to understand.

MOM   Let's just think about it a minute. Listen carefully and you can tell me what it means. "Every good thing bestowed and every perfect gift is from above, coming down from the Father of lights." I'll give you a hint: God is the Father of lights.

SUSIE   You mean everything good is from God?

MOM   That's right. This verse is a part of the Thanksgiving play because it reminds us that every good thing is from God, and we need to remember to thank him for every good gift.

SUSIE   You mean everything that is good comes directly from God?

MOM   Yes, Susie, this verse says *every* twice. We need to be reminded that every good thing comes from God so we don't take anything for granted. That's why Thanksgiving Day is so important. We need reminders to be thankful to God.

SUSIE   This *Pilgrim's Progress* is great. I understand half of this verse now.

MOM   The second half means God does not change. He is a good God, and he'll never change or vary, as your verse says: "With [God] there is no variation, or shifting shadow" (James 1:17 NASB).

SUSIE   Now I both understand and know the verse.

CHARLIE   *(Comes up and says in a deep voice)* Howdy, Pilgrim.

(MOM and SUSIE look at each other.)

SUSIE   Charlie, after the play tonight you won't be able to say that anymore.

CHARLIE   *(Laughs)* That's what you think, Pilgrim. I have a joke for you. If April showers bring May flowers, what do May flowers bring?

SUSIE   What?

CHARLIE   Pilgrims.

SUSIE and MOM   *(Laugh)*

MOM   That was funny, Charlie. We'd better start getting ready for the service. *(MOM leaves.)*

(CHARLIE and SUSIE start to walk off.)

SUSIE   Charlie, will you listen to my verse for tonight?

Easter: The Empty Tomb

Characters

Dad puppet
Mom puppet
Girl puppet
Boy puppet

(CHARLIE and DAD appear.)

CHARLIE   Dad, do I have to wear my new suit tomorrow? I feel like I'm in a monkey suit.

DAD   Now, Charlie, tomorrow is Easter Sunday, and we wanted you to have something special.

(SUSIE and MOM appear.)

SUSIE   Yes, I think my black shoes will go nicely with my new dress, and a pink belt and purse will be just perfect, and . . .

MOM   Wait a minute, Susie, you don't have a pink belt and purse.

SUSIE   I know, Mom, but you do!

CHARLIE   Good grief! I don't even want to wear my new monkey suit, but all Susie has talked about all week is her new clothes.

SUSIE   Well, Charlie, it's different with me. I'm making a fashion statement.

CHARLIE   *(Looks at audience.)* What a statement that will be!

SUSIE   What did you say?

CHARLIE   You'll be really pretty, just wait and see.

SUSIE   That's what I thought you said.

CHARLIE   I don't see what the big deal about Easter is, anyway. It just seems like another Sunday to me.

DAD   Charlie, Easter is very important. It is the day Christ rose from the dead.

CHARLIE   I know about that, but is it that important?

MOM   Charlie, it is very important. If Jesus hadn't risen from the dead, then people wouldn't have any hope of eternal life and living forever in heaven.

SUSIE   You mean if Jesus hadn't come back from the dead, people would not be able to go to heaven?

DAD   That's right, Susie.

SUSIE   Wow, then Easter is important!

DAD   Listen to this verse from the Bible which tells how important Easter is: 1 Corinthians 15:17: "And if Christ has not been raised, your faith is worthless; you are still in your sins" (NASB).

MOM   Easter is important because Jesus was raised from the dead; and it gives people the promise that when they die, they will be raised from the dead if they believe in Jesus.

CHARLIE   Boy, Easter is very important!

SUSIE   Easter is a lot more important than just wearing my new dress.

CHARLIE   Yes, I see. I don't think I'll wear my new suit.

DAD   Charlie, you can celebrate the real meaning of Easter and still wear your new suit.

SUSIE   Nice try, Charlie!

CHARLIE   Aw, shucks!